SOUTH-EAST
NORTHUMBERLAND
AT WAR 1939-45

SOUTH-EAST
NORTHUMBERLAND
AT WAR 1939-45

CRAIG ARMSTRONG

Pen & Sword
MILITARY

First published in Great Britain in 2019 by
PEN & SWORD MILITARY
An imprint of
Pen & Sword Books Ltd
Yorkshire – Philadelphia

ISBN 978 1 47386 7 468

A CIP catalogue record for this book is available from the British Library.

Printed and bound in England by TJ International, Padstow, Cornwall

Pen & Sword Books Limited incorporates the imprints of Atlas,
Archaeology, Aviation, Discovery, Family History, Fiction, History,
Maritime, Military, Military Classics, Politics, Select, Transport, True
Crime, Air World, Frontline Publishing, Leo Cooper, Remember When,
Seaforth Publishing, The Praetorian Press, Wharncliffe Local History,
Wharncliffe Transport, Wharncliffe True Crime and White Owl.

For a complete list of Pen & Sword titles please contact

PEN & SWORD BOOKS LIMITED
47 Church Street, Barnsley, South Yorkshire, S70 2AS, England
E-mail: enquiries@pen-and-sword.co.uk
Website: www.pen-and-sword.co.uk

Or

PEN AND SWORD BOOKS
1950 Lawrence Rd, Havertown, PA 19083, USA
E-mail: Uspen-and-sword@casematepublishers.com
Website: www.penandswordbooks.com

Contents

CHAPTER 1

1939: The Gathering Storm

Even before the outbreak of war, the government was putting in place plans for air raid precautions and civil defence. However, although the government was urging local authorities across the country to begin preparations as early as the mid-1930s many refused to take the matter seriously and progress stagnated. Whitley Bay Urban District Council (ARP Committee) recorded at its first meeting in October 1935 that it could make no decisions as to what steps should be taken as it lacked sufficient information to base any decisions upon.[1] Over the course of the next two years there were very few meetings held and so little or no action was taken to provide adequate ARP measures.

Until the Munich Crisis there were reportedly only seventeen or eighteen fully trained wardens to cover the whole area and this resulted in a subsequent problem with the provision of further training. The year 1938 saw several recruitment meetings, and, though attendance was high, there was very little subsequent interest in the enrolment forms that were distributed with only 5 per cent being completed and returned to the authorities.[2] The training of wardens was vital to the smooth functioning of the service. The wardens' role was complicated by the fact that, despite the example of the Spanish Civil War, no one in authority seemed to know what to expect and guidance from central government was minimal. In Whitley Bay and other areas in south-east Northumberland this resulted in the first classes concentrating largely on anti-gas warfare measures and methods to help the enforcement of the widely resented blackout. This led to a growing sense of disillusionment amongst the volunteers and to resentment from some of the local populace who viewed the wardens as being useless.

The government was keenly aware of other dangers from enemy bombing. It knew that in the event of incendiary raids the regular fire brigades would quickly find themselves overwhelmed. As a countermeasure to this a large and purely voluntary firefighting force, the Auxiliary Fire Service (AFS) was brought into being.[3] Paid at a roughly equal rate to the members of the regular brigades there was, at first, resentment of the 'amateurs'. To an extent this was understandable, the men of the AFS had never attended the scene of a fire; their duties in the early part of the war largely consisted of pumping out flooded shelters and they were completely inexperienced in firefighting duties. For many their first call-out would be on an actual incident involving very real risk to life. However, the AFS men did earn their wages as they were required to work forty-eight hours on duty, twenty-four hours off; the same as their regular colleagues. As well as this they were entitled to only limited sick pay and could be dismissed if they were not deemed to be fit enough to continue their duties.[4] The force was split between full-timers and part-time volunteers with the part-timers making up roughly 60 per cent of the total AFS manpower.[5] Recruitment to the AFS was initially slow but underwent something of a boom in the period immediately before the war, when it became clear that war was all but inevitable and that heavy bombing could probably be expected. In many parts of south-east Northumberland the creation of the AFS actually helped the firefighting situation as, given the large geographic area of the county, many smaller communities had lacked this ability before the war.

Flight Lieutenant John Sample had already made the local newspapers when he scored an early victory over a German bomber. A native of Longhirst, John, the son of Thomas Norman Sample and Kate Isabel Sample, had worked as a land agent in Morpeth for his uncle Mr W.C. Sample. A member of 607 (County Durham) Squadron of the Auxiliary Air Force since 1934 the outbreak of war had found him as a Flight Lieutenant in command of B Flight. On 10 September 1939, he took off in his Gladiator biplane fighter together with two others to search for enemy seaplanes off the north-east coast. The section discovered a Dornier Do 18 seaplane and severely damaged it before returning to base and claiming a probable victory. This was confirmed when the aircraft was forced to land in the sea alongside a British warship. In November 1939, 607 Squadron was posted to France.

By November, the extensions at Morpeth Cottage Hospital were ready to be opened and with the war situation it was anticipated that they might well be required for injured servicemen in the near future. On 25 November, the extension was officially opened by Mr R.C. Oliver, who went on to tour the site in the company of the Mayor of Morpeth, Councillor R. Elliott, and the matron of the hospital.

Demonstrating the risks run by the men of the AFS the first civilian fatality in south-east Northumberland (and indeed the north-east of England as a whole) was a member of the service. The sad event occurred on the night of 20 December when an appliance was on its way to a farm fire at Shotton near Plessey when it was in collision with an army lorry at Seaton Burn. Charles Rutherford, aged 45, of Fisher Lane, Gosforth, was killed while one of his colleagues lost a foot and another suffered a broken leg.

The dangers of driving in the blackout conditions had already been well highlighted by a rash of fatal accidents involving pedestrians and motor vehicles. Just days before the accident that claimed the life of Mr Rutherford, a West Sleekburn widow named Margaret White (65) was killed when she was

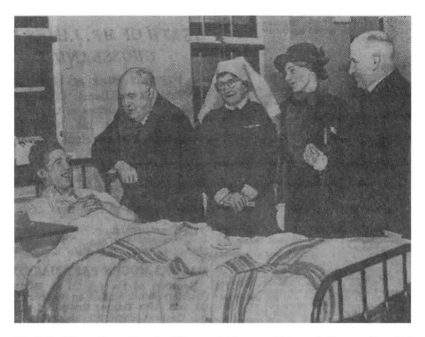

Mr R.C. Oliver, Councillor R. Elliott and Matron of Morpeth Cottage Hospital Touring New Extension of the Hospital. (The Journal)

hit by a bus at Stakeford while walking home after visiting a friend. In clear but very dark conditions, and with her torch batteries no longer working, Mrs White was apparently trying to cross the road when the bus hit her, killing her instantly. The coroner in recording a verdict of accidental death said that the accident was one of several recently, which demonstrated the need for pedestrians to use footpaths at night.

The blackout led to a huge number of early prosecutions for showing lights as magistrates were urged to stamp down on such offences and the police reacted with great zeal in prosecuting cases. At Whitley Bay court in December, for example, there were six cases heard. The most serious was an incident which occurred at Seghill Welfare Cinema. A special constable had seen a light outside and had told one of the men who worked there to turn it off. This was done but after walking away the constable noticed that it was switched back on. After ensuring the light was again turned off the constable reported the matter. In defence, the manager of the cinema, William Taylor Manderson, said that painters had been in and had turned the light on at the main switch. However, the magistrates found Mr Manderson guilty and fined him £2 1d. Other cases involved a miner from Hartford, a farm servant from East Holywell, a joiner and a grocer (both from Whitley Bay) and a farmer from Percy Main.

RAF Bomber Command had believed in the pre-war years that the new monoplane bombers at their disposal (especially the Wellington, Hampden and Blenheim) would be able, by flying in close formation, to defend themselves against enemy fighter attacks and the command entered the war with this belief still in place. On 14 December a force of forty-four aircraft made reconnaissance flights over the North Sea towards the Sylt area in search of enemy shipping. Amongst these was a flight of twelve Wellingtons which located a convoy north of Wilhemshaven. The weather was poor and the Wellingtons remained in the area at low level, unable to bomb, for some time, being attacked by anti-aircraft fire and enemy fighters with the result that five of their number were shot down. The RAF initially refused to believe the Luftwaffe's claim that its fighters had been responsible and, unwilling to let go of the theory of self-protecting bomber formations, preferred to believe that anti-aircraft fire was the more likely cause; this would have a tragic conclusion.

Four days later, a formation of twenty-four Wellingtons were sent on a similar mission but ordered not to descend below 10,000ft so as to avoid the worst of the anti-aircraft fire. Although two aircraft turned back early the remainder spotted an enemy convoy and attacked from 13,000ft. However, they had been monitored from 70 miles away by an experimental radar set and enemy Messerschmitt ME109s were vectored onto them. Their formation partially disrupted by anti-aircraft fire, the bombers proved easy prey and twelve were quickly shot down for the loss of only two fighters. Amongst the men to lose their lives was 19-year-old Aircraftman Second Class Isaac Davidson Leighton of East Cramlington. Leighton was flying as a Wireless Operator/Air Gunner in Wellington IA (N2961) of 149 Squadron. Just before 9.30 am the crew, piloted by Flying Officer M.F. Briden, had taken off from their base at Mildenhall and set course. Severely damaged by enemy fighters over the target area the crew had turned for home but were forced to ditch the aircraft when 40-60 miles off Cromer. Although at least three men were seen clinging to a dinghy and despite an extensive search operation no survivors were found.[6] For Aircraftman Leighton's family an anxious wait ensued which was ended when confirmation of the youngster's death was received in February 1940.[7] The tragic events of 18 December led many within Bomber Command to privately concede that the idea of a self-defending daylight bomber formation was flawed and eventually led to a realisation that a substantial change in policy was necessary.

The first wartime Christmas was one in which people attempted to carry on as normal. However, the presence of evacuees played a considerable role in many communities and this, along with some shortages, served to keep the war at the forefront of peoples' minds. There were parties held for the staff and pupils of three Tyneside schools who had been evacuated to Morpeth. The staff and children, from Cragside Infants' School and Royal Jubilee

Infants' School in Newcastle and Linskill Infants' School in North Shields, were entertained by the staff and pupils of Dacre Street School where the evacuees took part in singing, dancing and games before a tea party. This was followed by the 'climax of a most hilarious afternoon' when the evacuees were presented with presents from under the Christmas tree by Santa Claus.[8]

The next day, the staff and children from Cragside School were entertained by Councillor James Doherty and the staff and pupils of St Robert's Roman Catholic School. Once again the entertainment consisted of a tea with singing and dancing followed by each evacuee being given some fruit to take home to their billet. After this party the staff of both schools enjoyed their own party and tea. The generosity of Morpethians earned high praise from the staff and children of the guest schools.

In Ashington there were widespread efforts to ensure that children enjoyed Christmas despite the war. A large number of events, ranging from tea parties to dances, were being organised locally, with the services and ARP services playing a considerable role. Typical of the larger parties which took place was that which was organised and hosted by the Ideal Service Stores. The party took place at the Methodist Central Hall and saw 350 children treated to tea and a film show. The highlight, once again, was the appearance of Santa Claus who gave out 350 boxes of sweets and an equal number of oranges. Even here, however, the war intervened when 'One tiny guest, taking Santa Claus seriously solemnly requested that he be supplied with a sword at Christmas.'[9] The staff of one of Ashington's first aid posts decided to hold their own Christmas party, complete with tree, to fight the boredom of spending the Christmas season on duty. While admitting that in some households the celebrations would be muted because of news of early casualties the local press insisted that for most the celebrations would continue as normal, albeit behind the blackout curtains. Indeed, one of the main features of this first wartime Christmas was a lack of crowds of last-minute present hunters thronging the streets as most avoided 'venturing abroad at night under the blackout conditions'.[10] Despite this and other hardships, the newspapers were sure that the party spirit and gaiety would be maintained and perhaps even heightened because of the war, although it would be against a background of sadness and anxiety about the future.

Certainly the shops continued to advertise their wares to an eager public during the season while, in contrast to the First World War, the people of south-east Northumberland were exhorted to enjoy a Christmas beer (or two). It is clear from the local press that the well-known firms of G. Rutherford & Co. Ltd. and Mason & Co. Ltd of Morpeth and G. Arrowsmith of Ashington ran adverts encouraging consumers to shop throughout the Christmas period. Elsewhere, however, were adverts which showed the darker side of a wartime Christmas with at least one advert from an Ashington firm for mourning clothing.

The newspapers also ran columns throughout December which gave advice on how to prepare treats for Christmas with ingredients that were still easily obtainable. Many of these recipes were wartime twists on Christmas classics. One correspondent, Jane Lanchester, wrote giving four such recipes: grapefruit glace; banana trifle; Christmas gingerbread and apple rose cake. Prices had begun to increase for many foodstuffs and many an anxious housewife would have welcomed these handy tips to provide for their family.

Average Prices in 1939.

Item	Price
Butter (lb)	1s 6d
Margarine (lb)	6d
Lard (lb)	7d
Cheddar Cheese (lb)	10d
Danish Bacon (lb)	1s 6d
Milk (pt)	3d
Sugar (lb)	4½d
Nestle Cream (small tin)	6½d
Sweet Biscuits (lb)	1s
Chocolate Fingers (lb)	1s 9d
Flour (stone)	1s 7d
Self-Raising Flour (3lbs)	7½d
Danish Eggs (doz)	2s
Potatoes (stone)	1s 2d
Jaffa Oranges (each)	1d
Pears (lb)	4d
McIntosh Red Apples (lb)	4d
Grapefruit (5)	4d
Lemons (each)	½d
Cooking Apples (3½lb)	6d

Eating is certainly an integral part of Christmas but for the people of wartime south-east Northumberland entertainment also featured high on the agenda, with local cinemas seeing a good trade throughout the season. In Morpeth, the Playhouse had a varied showing with Christmas Eve showings of *Call of the Yukon* (1938) starring Richard Arlen and *Call of the Leathernecks* (1938) starring Richard Cromwell, while Christmas night featured *The Last of the Cavalry* (released as *Army Girl*) (1938) starring Preston Foster. The main competitor to the Playhouse, the Coliseum, meanwhile was showing

Romance of the Limberlost (1938) starring Jean Parker and boxing drama *The Fifth Round* (1938) starring Frankie Darro; while on Christmas Day the entertainment was provided by topical spy thriller *Secret Journey* (1939) starring Basil Radford and Sylvia St Claire.

A feature of this first wartime Christmas was the high attendance at places of worship and the eagerness of the clergy to provide some form of moral and spiritual comfort for people during the crisis.

CHAPTER 2

1940: The Storm Breaks

January was marked by heavy snowfall, which at times caused severe disruption on the roads and railways. Throughout mid-January there were repeated complaints to local councillors that the authorities were not doing enough to clear snow away from roads, which were dangerous as a result. Reacting to this the local councils agreed to employing extra men to supervise either temporary workers or volunteers in order to cope.

One effect of the snowfall was that the issue of respirators for infants between 2 and 4 years of age had been delayed in places as people were correctly reluctant to bring such young children out into the cold to wait at distribution points and so the deliveries had to take place on an individual basis. The hope was expressed that with the clearing of roads the distribution of the respirators to local dispersal points could begin.

As the miserable weather continued throughout January, the crowds taking advantage of the entertainment on offer at local cinemas grew. In Morpeth in mid-January two picture houses, The Playhouse and The Coliseum, offered a wide range of action, adventure, westerns and comedy shows. Popular regular characters such as Charlie Chan, Tarzan, Dr Kildare, the Cisco Kid and Laurel and Hardy featured heavily, with parts played by such stalwarts as Sidney Toler, Warner Baxter, Johnny Weissmuller, Maureen O'Sullivan, Lionel Barrymore, Rosalind Russell and Kermit Maynard.

At the same time shops in the small towns of south-east Northumberland were advertising their January sales in the hope of attracting custom as per usual. Rutherford's of Morpeth advertised a variety of articles of clothing including khaki shirts which were 'suitable for Officers' wear' and Arrowsmith's of Ashington promised 'Values Impossible to Repeat!' and 'Genuine Price Reductions' on a wide variety of clothing, linens and household fabrics, while at the same time urging its customers to 'Shop Early. Shop in Daylight'.[11] The Morpeth firm of John Smail & Sons offered bedroom suites, Chesterfield suites, dining suites, bedsteads and bedding all at pre-war prices, which it claimed was an overall saving of 25 per cent along with free delivery for all items but cautioned that customers should hurry as the pre-war prices would not last.

Despite the determination of many to try to go about their lives normally as far as was possible in the circumstances, the men and women of the ARP services were aware that the Phoney War might not continue and that their services might be required. Because of this the winter period saw constant training at both a national and local level with many drills and exercises taking place. Typical of the local efforts was an exercise held in mid-January in the Seaton Valley area. This involved a fictitious raid which led to twenty separate incidents requiring the attendance of firemen, rescue squads and/or decontamination squads. Because of the fractured nature of the creation of ARP units in many areas, such exercises were vital to ensure that separate groups could work together. In this case the exercise involved fire and rescue squads from six separate locations and groups under the central control of Seaton Delaval Depot. Those involved were from Earsdon, Klondyke, Seghill Colliery, Backworth Colliery, Hartley Main Colliery group and Cramlington Co-operative Society ARP section. Lessons learned from the exercise were passed on to all ARP sections by the chair of the Northumberland ARP committee, Councillor M.J. Mall. Another example of this growing awareness of the necessity of training was shown by the difficulties experienced in the messaging system in the Whitley Bay area. As a result of this first exercise a further one was held in May 1940 and from the results it was determined that there were several forms of messages that were unnecessary and resulted in confusion and delays. These message formats were discontinued and the service improved as a result.[12]

We have already seen how some ARP and civil defence services were completely unprepared for the war and it appears that in some parts of the area this also applied to the AFS. Clearly the AFS would be a vital service in the event of future air raids but equipping the force was problematic from the outset. A year into the war and in the Whitley Bay area there were only two purpose-built fire engines bolstered by some eighteen trailer pumps of varying capacities and serviceability.[13]

As well as the wardens the members of anti-gas and decontamination teams were also an ever-present reminder of the situation and the probability of aerial attack. While they did not have to perform their main duties they were still an active part of the ARP services. As the war continued the decontamination squads were increasingly expected to perform debris clearance and other ARP duties.[14] During the early stages of the war, however, people were still anxious about the possibility of gas attacks and this led to the squads being called out on several occasions. In what was a fairly common mistake Whitley Bay's decontamination squad and gas identification squad were both called out in September 1940 after a report of someone smelling phosgene gas. Geraniums in a neighbouring garden's flower bed were later established to be responsible for the alarm.[15]

The early establishment and strength of the decontamination squads demonstrates just how seriously the threat of gas attack was taken by the local authorities. The fact that they were maintained until the end of the war demonstrates that the continuing risk of a last ditch chemical retaliatory attack by Germany was taken seriously in the local ARP community. The decontamination squads represent an example of how both central and local government was unable accurately to predict the likely events of an air attack and how efficiently some local authorities were preparing for all eventualities, no matter what the cost.

Despite the increasing tempo of ARP training, in many ways normal life continued – even considering the precarious position in which Britain found itself. The familiar family routines of weddings, christening and funerals continued along with some of the traditional events and customs of the area. Weddings in Northumberland had developed a wide range of customs including brides having to jump over stools and the presence of local children at the exits to the churchyard demanding a 'toll' to allow the new couple to pass.

This was not the experience of every community, however. At Whitley Bay the local authority's mortuary services received early practise when four bodies, two seamen and two Luftwaffe airmen, were washed onto the shore early in the year.[16] These four bodies would be the first of a steady stream to be brought ashore at south-east Northumberland coastal communities such as Blyth, Newbiggin and Whitley Bay.

Despite the war, the annual Morpeth hiring fair for agricultural workers went ahead on 6 March. There was a good attendance and it was reported that a fair amount of business was done but that many of the people who attended

Morpeth Hiring Fair. (The Sphere)

had already found work through newspaper advertisements and that many of them, and townspeople, attended because of the covered fair which took place in the New Market Place.

A common feature of the home front during the First World War was the disputes between social classes over the matter of the consumption of alcohol with many in the upper strata of society seeming to believe that the working classes could not be expected to control their drinking habits. In March there was evidence that some elements of society evidently still believed this to be the case. The licensee of the Black Swan on King Street in Morpeth made an application to the Brewster Sessions for the licence to be transferred from the King Street premises to a newly erected building at Stobhillgate. The primary reason for this was that recent slum clearances in the town had affected the King Street site and there were now some 300 houses at Stobhillgate with a further 80 more to be built with no provision of public houses (the nearest being The Newcastle Hotel and the Sun Inn, both of which were over half a mile away). A census of those adults living in the area had come back with an overwhelming vote in favour of the new building being granted a licence (93 per cent voted in favour with only 1 per cent objecting to the licence). The local police did not object given that the plans which had been submitted to them met with their approval and it seems to have been relatively straight forward. However, representatives from several religious groups were present to make their objections plain. These objectors included the Congregational Church, Church of England, Howard Terrace Methodist Church and St George's Presbyterian Church. Speaking on behalf of the objectors the Reverend Baty of the Congregational Church said that the people in Stobhill had been removed from the slums to begin a new life in more comfortable and healthier surroundings and that the presence of a public house would provide unnecessary temptation and could lead to them not making the best of the new opportunity they had been afforded. He said that he and his fellow objectors felt that the presence of 'a public house there would provide very undesirable encouragement to drink on the part of those who are really anxious to keep alcoholic liquor away from them. A licence up there would be an inducement to people to drink,' The Reverend Baty continued, by hinting that if the transfer was granted, parents in Stobhillgate, instead of providing for their children and new homes, would spend money on drink. He also claimed that the churches, in co-operation with the Salvation Army and the council, were attempting to organise healthier alternatives for recreation in Stobhillgate but gave no details of these. After adjourning for a short private deliberation of the case the chair returned and said that after careful consideration he was granting the transfer of licence.

As casualties continued to mount, the announcements in local newspaper rolls of honour became commonplace for many communities. The coastal colliery village of Lynemouth learned that one of its townsfolk had lost his life while flying with RAF Coastal Command. On 13 April Leading Aircraftman Thomas Liddle was flying as an air gunner in Lockheed Hudson I (N7323 ZS-Y) of 233 Squadron. Taking off shortly before 1.45 pm from RAF Leuchars for an operation to Stavanger they were shot down off Stavanger by a Messerschmitt ME-110 piloted by Unteroffizier Bruckner of ZG76 and the four man crew were all killed. The crew, including LAC Liddle were buried in Sola Churchyard, Norway.[17]

As the war entered its second year, many Northumbrians had been left puzzled by the lack of military action and the Phoney War (also commonly known as the Bore War) had become a topic of much debate on the streets, with some expressing the hope that the war could be halted. Such hopes were dashed, however, when Germany invaded Norway and Denmark in April. The British response to the invasion of Norway was an organisational shambles and a demoralised British force was forced to retreat. The Norwegian campaign had huge ramifications including a two-day debate in the House of Commons which resulted in Neville Chamberlain narrowly winning a vote of confidence but losing his mandate to continue as prime minister. After talks with his own party and the Labour Party leadership, Chamberlain resigned on 10 May.

Chamberlain's resignation coincided with the assessment of enemy aliens who were forced before tribunals which sorted them into three categories (A, B and C) with the first being interned for the duration, the second group being released but with restrictions on their activities and where they could live or travel and the third group (which was the majority) being released completely.

On the same day that Britain lost its prime minister, the Germans crossed the border into Belgium and Holland and, using fast-moving tank columns backed up by supporting airpower and artillery, made massive and rapid gains. In the south the German blitzkrieg pushed through Luxembourg and the Ardennes Forest to bypass the much-vaunted Maginot Line and the Germans reached the coast in just eleven days, cutting off the BEF in the north. Despite brave and indeed heroic resistance, the BEF was forced back and it became clear that, unless an evacuation could be made, Britain would lose the majority of her army.

The news of the events in France and the Low Countries was met with barely suppressed horror amongst the civilian population of Northumberland and there were widespread recriminations against the perceived mismanagement of the Chamberlain government. Nevertheless, morale was reported to be holding and as it became clear that the evacuations from Dunkirk had been successful beyond anyone's imagining a feeling grew of determination to oppose Hitler and Nazism no matter what.

With the Germans now poised across the Channel and occupying Norway, the people of Northumberland became even more acutely aware of the possibilities of air raids. On the night of 25/26 June the sirens wailed over south-east Northumberland and people took to the shelters. The raid was actually a very small one with bombs dropped over three locations. At West Chevington over thirty incendiaries were scattered over the fields of Whitefields Farm causing little or no damage; at Longhorsley six high-explosive bombs fell at Linden Farm with the only victim being a sheep, while at Spital Point, Newbiggin, a single HE fell causing no conclusive damage.

With increasing fears over the possibility of invasion from either air or sea many of those who could not join the armed forces, ranging from those who were too old or young to those who were in reserved occupations, began to ever more determinedly press the point that they should be allowed to make a contribution to the defence of Britain. On 14 May, the Secretary of State for War, Anthony Eden, made a broadcast on the BBC asking for those who wished to play a role in the defence of Britain, but who were unable to enlist, to volunteer for service in a new force which was to be known as the Local Defence Volunteers (LDV). Eden's broadcast asked for those between 17 and 65 to join the LDVs and promised that the force would be uniformed and armed. Those who were interested were instructed to give their names at the local police station. The government expected between 200,000 and 500,000 men to register but within weeks nearly 1,500,000 had registered their interest.

Local authorities in south-east Northumberland were generally keen to help in any way they could, with training areas and drill halls quickly being secured. In Morpeth, for example, the mayor, who was a keen supporter of the force, praised the local populace for coming forward in such encouraging numbers and the council made 40 acres of the North Common available to the force for training. Police stations, many of which had had little or no warning, coped with large numbers of men eager to be of service in the defence of Britain.

The regional organisation of the LDV was left in the hands of the Regional Commissioners for Civil Defence, the Lord Lieutenants and the local territorial organisations. Sir Arthur Lambert, the Regional Commissioner for the Northern district, was a keen supporter of the force and commented the day after the announcement of its formation that it was of 'essential importance' and it was of 'supreme necessity that its numbers should be maintained at adequate strength'. Showing the confusion over the role of the LDV that reigned for the first months of the force Sir Arthur even referred to the volunteers as 'the Anti-Parachute Defence Troops' and said that he was sure that men would come forward in 'an impressive rush' as everyone 'feels at this moment the surging impulse to do what lies in their power to help the national effort'. He also commented that it was the typical reaction of the British people to a 'pestilential bully' to grow even more grimly determined and to resist with such force as to drive Germany 'back on to his knees whining for an armistice' as had happened in 1918.[18]

Numbers of Volunteers for the LDV by midday on 15 May.

Town	Numbers
Whitley Bay	250
Ashington	100
Blyth	87
Bedlington	85
Morpeth	56
Newbiggin	50
Total	628

The stream of volunteers remained steady throughout the week after the announcement of the formation of the LDV with 1,100 names being registered at Bedlington in just five days.

Sir Arthur was keenly aware of the potential for trained ARP personnel deserting their posts for what they perceived as the potentially more active LDV. He reminded those thousands of people throughout the region who had signed up for ARP duties at the outset, been trained, but had since withdrawn from the scheme largely due to the lack of action during the Phoney War to once again come forward as the ARP services were likely to be stretched to the utmost in the near future. He went on to urge people to re-join or to volunteer as it would be a source of regret if they were left as 'untrained and unhelpful onlookers during enemy attacks'.

In keeping with the spirit of the time the *Morpeth Herald*'s military correspondent wrote a column at the end of May which presented descriptions of the appearance and tactics of German paratroopers so that 'everyone in the county' could become familiar with them and recognise such a landing. The correspondent gave five key objectives of paratroop forces which included the following:

1. The organisation and arming of local Fifth Column members.
2. To sow panic and confusion amongst the civilian population especially through the spreading of false news.
3. To disrupt lines of communication.
4. To damage or destroy key locations such as bridges, power stations, telephone exchanges, stores and ammunition dumps.
5. To provide information to their air force by signalling them.

Clearly the correspondent was amongst those who were fearful of a suspected fifth column and assumed that enemy paratroopers would not only fulfil a military role but also a psychological one in reducing the morale of the British people. He went on to recommend that the best way of preventing such landings from being successful was constant patrolling and speed of reaction in local areas. He also cautioned that such paratroopers were not always in uniform and that they often had detailed information on the local area, which had been provided by fifth columnists. In addition, the correspondent also highlighted the possibility that the fifth column also had female members in order to appear less suspicious.

Demonstrating limited understanding of what had happened during airborne landings in Holland the correspondent stated that the first wave of parachutists 'were mostly young men of the desperado type armed with machine pistols, and apparently members of the Hitler Youth and party organisations'. Showing a failure to appreciate the determination and skill of the German army he said that subsequent waves consisted of young soldiers many of whom were unwilling and fearful and 'had to be forcibly ejected from the planes'. He correctly argued that a prime target would be airfields and urged civilians to report any suspicious aircraft to 'the well-armed groups of our defence volunteers'. His estimation of the arms available to the LDV were obviously erroneous but he clearly rated the force highly saying that most of the LDV were 'old soldiers and first-class marksmen'.[19] While it is true that a high proportion of the LDV were indeed former servicemen, (estimates put the average at around 35 per cent), many were not and the ability to use their weapons had not yet been ascertained in most cases. In any case the vast majority were not armed at this stage as modern weapon production was taken up by the regular army which had lost so much of its equipment in France.

One role that the LDV/Home Guard played was in aiding regular troops in manning local defences. Defences were quickly constructed around the vulnerable coastlines of Britain and were further developed while the threat remained (throughout 1940-42). Of particular concern in Northumberland was Druridge Bay, which features a large gently sloping sandy beach backed by sand dunes pierced at several points by small streams allowing access off the beach to the road and coastal farmland beyond. The site was seen as being 'exceptionally vulnerable to an enemy landing [and was] ... the most critical point (the Centre Sub-Sector of No 2 Sector) in the defence positions occupied by 162 Infantry Brigade'.[20]

The 162nd Infantry Brigade, under the command of Brigadier J. Macready and, from the end of August, Brigadier R.B.S. Reford, was responsible for the defence of the entire Northumberland coast and was thus spread quite thin, but it was bolstered by local Home Guard units. A territorial formation and part of the 54th (East Anglian) Infantry Division (another territorial unit) the brigade included: 6th Battalion, Bedfordshire and Hertfordshire Regiment; 1st Battalion, Hertfordshire Regiment; 2nd Battalion, Hertfordshire Regiment; and 162nd Infantry Brigade Anti-Tank Company. The defences at Druridge Bay were extensive and included minefields, anti-tank ditches, pillboxes, sandbagged positions, anti-tank blocks, beach scaffolding (with mines), and anti-tank artillery positions. Just inland from Druridge was a very unusual example of a disguised pillbox which was constructed to appear as a deserted, tumble-down, cottage while the defences also included a loop-holed wall in a section of a Knights Templar preceptory at Chibburn.

There were other vulnerable locations on the coast of south-east Northumberland and defences were constructed throughout 1940 and 1941 at these sites. Yet another gently sloping beach which was ideal for enemy landings ran from Blyth to Seaton Sluice. Possibly this beach might be even more appealing to the Germans as it was closer to Newcastle and lay between two ports (Blyth and the smaller one at Seaton Sluice) which could be seized as well as having several airfields just inland. As a result of this vulnerability defences were built along this stretch. They consisted of anti-aircraft positions, anti-tank blocks, anti-tank gun positions, beach defences, coastal defence batteries, pillboxes, roadblocks, searchlight emplacements and trenches.

The small port of Seaton Sluice was defended by a series of positions including at least four pillboxes: one of these was a relatively unusual concrete sandbag type. The majority of pillboxes found in the county were of the lozenge type but there were others that were used in specific circumstances such as the above-mentioned concrete sandbag and the disguised type (a further example of which was found at Gloster Hill, south of Warkworth) and also rectangular examples which were proven to be very vulnerable to enemy fire (one such was at Newbiggin). Very close to the harbour at Hartley was the site of a Chain Home Low radar site. This was built on the site of the First World War-era Robert's Battery and featured extensive underground facilities, a command post with combined officers' quarters (now a private residence called Fort House) and several stretches of loop-holed walls (including possibly the country's only defended toilet).

Other defences included the establishment of a number of so-called 'stop lines' which ran along several Northumbrian rivers and other natural features. These were the Coquet stop line, which ran from upper Coquetdale to Amble, the Wansbeck stop line, which ran to the west and east of Morpeth, the Alnwick-Wooler stop line, and the Belford-Wooler stop line. Along these lines, various towns and villages became nodal points of defence and received particular attention from military planners. The market town of Morpeth was one such location and a ring of defences were thrown up around the town (which lay on a main north-south road and the east coast line) consisting largely of loop-holed walls, pillboxes and roadblocks.

As the war news worsened, there was an increase in tension with many Northumbrians beginning to exhibit more vociferous anti-alien sentiment. There were growing press calls to 'intern the lot' and demands that those aliens who had been placed in categories B and C to be rounded up and interned too. Though understandable these attitudes were often illogical as many enemy aliens had fled to Britain to avoid persecution in their home countries while others had lived in the area for many years and were naturalised. By the end of May, tempers had flared in several communities and there were incidents of vandalism against properties perceived to be owned by enemy aliens. The entry of Italy into the war on the side of the Axis on 10 June increased the tension. Britain was prepared for this eventuality and within hours of Mussolini's speech the police began rounding up Italians and those of Italian descent. On 12 May, the government ordered the internment of male aliens who were living in vulnerable coastal areas such as Blyth and followed this just four days later with the internment of all category B aliens. By the end of June the police were told that they should act to detain any category C German or Austrians about whom they had doubts.

On 12 June there was an incident in Morpeth in which the premises of an Italian confectioner were attacked by two local men. The proprietor of the shop (at 4 Newgate Street), Mr Giuseppe Resteghini, had been interned on 10 June, leaving his wife and her sister in charge of the shop. Shortly before 11.00 pm two plate glass windows were smashed when half bricks were thrown through them. Two local butchers, Thomas Alfred Stait (42) of Grange View, Newgate Street, and Robert Croudace (35) of 9 Hood Street, were observed by a special constable, Frederick Jobson, outside the shop and he gave evidence that they appeared to have thrown something at the windows. After detaining the men Constable Jobson sent for the police who took the men to the station. Margaret Carter, Mr Resteghini's sister-in-law, stated that after the windows had broken she had seen the two accused outside the shop with one looking like he had just thrown something. A customer, George Alexander Hankin, gave evidence that when he and his wife left the shop shortly after 10.00 pm he was spoken to by Mr Croudace who accused him of being unpatriotic in using a shop owned by an enemy of the country. In the subsequent argument Mr Hankin said that he was convinced that the men intended to create some disturbance so, after seeing his wife home, he returned and spoke to them cautioning them that 'it would be a cowardly action to wreck the shop if they intended to do so as there were only two young girls and a boy in the shop and that … it would not do any good if they did wreck the shop'. Mr Hankin stated that Mr Stait replied that 'if it did no good it would do no harm'.

When taken to the police station the two men denied having anything to do with the incident but admitted that they had been drinking in several public houses that evening. However, with nothing else to go on but witness testimony, the men were released but told that inquiries would continue. The police later traced the thrown brick to a pile at the gasworks and given that Mr Croudace lived near there he would have had access to the brick pile. Because of this the men were interviewed again and subsequently charged – but refused to say anything. Mr Charles Webb, acting for the defendants, said that Mr Hankin's testimony should be discounted as the defendants had made no mention of wrecking the shop and this suggestion had come from Mr Hankin because of what he had witnessed in the last war. It was also argued that there was bad feeling between Special Constable Jobson and Mr Stait as the latter had once worked for Jobson, who was also a butcher, and had been sacked and, as a result, was now unemployed. Mr Stait conceded that he had accused Mr Hankin of being unpatriotic and added that he had a son in the services who might 'be sent to fight these people'. Both Stait and Croudace denied that they had smashed the windows and said that there were other people on the street at the time who could have been responsible.[21]

The prosecutor, Mr T.D. Shaw, stated that he believed that the two men had taken the decision to smash the shop windows because of Italy's entry into the war and [they] believed that they were justified in doing so. Mr Shaw also pointed out that the property was not owned by Mr Resteghini and was in fact rented from Mrs Edith Burn (who was a baker and pastry cook with premises at 42 and 44 Bridge Street). Given the evidence the bench found little difficulty in finding the men guilty. Croudace was fined the sum of £2 and ordered to pay £5 in compensation while Mr Stait was fined £1 and ordered to pay £3 damages.[22]

With the urgency of maintaining the supply of coal the already very dangerous work of the miner became even more perilous and tragic accidents were a feature of the wartime mining industry in south-east Northumberland. In May, a young man from Barrington lost his life at Bomarsund Pit. The unfortunate miner, Thomas Barnes Mitcheson (25), was killed when the seam he was trying to expand collapsed onto him. An experienced miner, Mitcheson had shored up the seam with timber in a manner which the shift deputy agreed seemed to be secure enough. The deputy had been warned by his colleague who had worked the previous shift that in that particular seam 'there was going to be trouble – a fault'. Having observed the fault, the deputy, William Robinson, visited Mitcheson several times during the shift and warned him to be extremely careful. At around 4.30 pm he was told that the shaft had collapsed upon Mitcheson. When he reached the scene of the collapse Mitchesons's colleagues had dug him out but on examination it was found that he was dead. Upon being questioned during the subsequent coroner's inquest Mr Robinson estimated that over half a ton of stone and coal had fallen on the unfortunate miner. This led the coroner to state that despite the fact that 'Mitcheson was a careful workman and a man of experience' his death was due to the shoring timbers giving way and recorded a verdict of accidental death.[23]

It was not only machinery that could cause injury or death: the continued heavy use of pit ponies could also prove to be dangerous work. In June, a 39-year-old miner from Cowpen Colliery, Alfred Rumsby, was admitted to a Newcastle hospital after suffering injuries resulting from being dragged by a pony, which had taken fright and bolted.

In November, a 25-year-old Blyth miner named Albert Ivan Charles Webb was fatally injured while working at the Bates Pit. Mr Webb was a rolleywayman who worked on the rail lines used for moving the tubs of coal from the pit and, because of his working conditions, he was using a stay to hold the tubs in place but when he removed the stay it swung around and struck him in the stomach causing internal injuries. Mr Webb refused to lie on a stretcher and instead walked to the ambulance which conveyed him to hospital where unfortunately he died.

For many of the mining communities of south-east Northumberland the local miners' institutes were centres for recreation and learning. Many of the institutes had extensive sports facilities along with reading rooms and lending libraries. One of the largest, at Ashington, in addition to a billiards room and lending library also had a swimming baths, bowling greens, tennis courts and a ladies' room. However, even popular facilities such as these were adversely affected by the war and in March the institute announced that there had been a financial loss over the previous year and membership numbers had declined. The institute admitted that it was spending some £358 per annum (over £18,000 today) above its earnings while membership had fallen to 1,751: largely due to the large numbers who joined the services. However, they also reported that the majority of facilities continued to be very well attended, with the library and the swimming baths being particularly popular. During the course of the year some 5,541 books had been loaned out and four members were given certificates by the Royal Life Saving Society. However, several swimming tests, school competitions and the institute's annual concert had been cancelled due to the war.

The miners and colliery workers were keenly aware of their former colleagues who had joined up and were now facing the enemy. In many pits, collections were taken up to give support for these men. At the Maude Pit, Backworth, the miners agreed to a levy of 2d per week for adults and 1d per week for boys (who still made up a considerable part of the workforce) to raise funds for those former miners at the Maude Pit who had joined the army.

Even before summer the people of south-east Northumberland were being urged to lay in an additional stock of coal both to boost the industry (which had been hard hit by the start of the war) and, in the event of a hard winter, to ensure that they had adequate supplies in case the supply network, already strained by the war effort, broke down in poor weather.

The collieries of the area had a strong tradition of maintaining brass bands and amidst fears that such organisations would be seen as an unpatriotic luxury during wartime the bands of several collieries came up with the idea of holding public competitions in the various towns, which would raise funds for the Northumberland & Durham War Needs Fund. The expenses of hosting the competitions and of providing prizes was borne by the hosting band committee and the events were in fact very successful. The round held at Newbiggin-by-the-Sea attracted a particularly strong crowd with an estimated 600 spectators attending. Featuring bands from Bedlington, Cambois, Cowpen, Lynemouth, Newbiggin, Netherton and North Seaton the competition was hosted in the modern cinema of the Wallaw (Newbiggin) Biograph Company (for free) and was won by North Seaton, with Netherton finishing second, Bedlington third and the hosts fourth. Councillor J. Adams, who presided over the contest, said that it was a very praiseworthy scheme and that in 'keeping workmen's bands in action in war-time' was a worthwhile activity since it boosted morale as well as raising funds.[24]

As shortages became ever more acute the willingness of people to, in the words of the famous campaign, 'dig for victory' increased and although many were already producing vegetables some were eager to go even further and, encouraged by the government, began to raise hens and pigs. Pig clubs were soon being formed by groups of workers in rural and urban areas of the county with communities combining to raise the animals for essential additions to the meat ration. One such club was formed at Erlington House, Clousden Hill, Longbenton, by workmen employed by Longbenton Urban District Council.[25]

Despite the numbers of people raising pigs, the concerns over scarcity of bacon and other supplies was a topic of conversation by November, when people in the Morpeth area were reported to be suffering from severe shortages. The issue was raised with the local authorities being told that people were on short rations for bacon, and asked 'where is the bacon?' The local press seemed to be in agreement and highlighted problems with other items by saying that the cynically minded believed this was a similar situation to onions which, since being price controlled, 'were as scarce as strawberries in winter'.[26]

As the war went on and shortages began to impact on the population of the area those who were arranging charity collections had to find ever more creative methods to raise funds. One sure-fire way was to provide some form of entertainment and the Sleekburn Red Cross committee was praised for putting on a concert featuring the singers of the Bebside Male Voice Choir and a number of female guest opera artistes accompanied by Morpeth pianist Gladys Willis at the Wallaw Picture House in Bedlington. The concert saw the picture house full to capacity and a substantial sum raised. The organisers thanked the staff of the picture house and the artistes for their contributions adding 'It is this spirit of service for such a worthy object, so ungrudgingly given, which makes us proud of this dear country of ours.'[27]

The first wartime Easter was a period for reflection on the wartime situation but also an opportunity to raise more money for the war effort and for humanitarian efforts. In Morpeth, a dance held at the Parochial Hall on Easter Monday raised the sum of £10 18s 6d for the Red Cross and St John War Fund and resulted in letters of thanks from the Mayor, Alderman R. Elliott, to the organiser, Mr Percy R. Soulsby and to the YMCA for agreeing to the use of the hall. Meanwhile, on Wednesday, 27 March, St George's Hospital, Morpeth, held a whist drive in aid of war work, which raised further sums. The war workers of St George's had already volunteered their services as a work party and had supplied several hundred knitted garments to the forces. The nurses and other workers at local hospitals used money raised locally not only to buy medical supplies but also to purchase items such as stationery for those who found themselves far from relatives.

Just days later, the Parochial Hall hosted an Easter tea and bring and buy sale, which attracted a large number of the congregation: over 250 people attended the tea. The Reverend J.M. Paulin praised the people of Morpeth for turning out in such numbers to support the work of the church despite the wartime situation. The tea was followed by the almost inevitable whist drive and by an evening dance with music supplied by The Collegians.

In the village of Ulgham, the Easter weekend also saw fundraising activities with the traditional parishioners' sale of work and tea at the Women's Institute hut. The event was opened by Lady Joicey of Ford Castle and she praised the people of the village in her opening speech saying that, despite the war and the concerns it brought, the activities of the church had to go on. She also praised the many women of the village who were keenly knitting and sewing garments for the men in the forces. Lady Joicey, perhaps reflecting the earlier experience of conflict, actually referred to the men as being 'in the trenches'. The event was a great success and was followed by a whist drive and, in the evening, by the Easter night dance held for the local young people who were entertained by the music of the Merrymakers' Dance Band.

The knitting of woollen garments for servicemen was a common charitable activity across the area and a great many large and small organisations took part. The increasing cost of wool meant that many smaller groups began to struggle during the latter part of the year. One such group was the Morpeth Mothers' Union. By November, the union had contributed over 900 garments to the Northumberland & Durham War Needs Committee but was forced to make a series of appeals for donations to cover the cost of wool. The people of the area responded generously and monetary donations began to pour into the treasurer (Mrs E. Appleby of The Farm, St George's Hospital), the secretary (Mrs F. Rutherford of 'Burnmarsh', Mitford Road) and to Mrs Baker of The Rectory, Morpeth.

As was the case in the previous war the people of south-east Northumberland remained keen to contribute their money to the war effort. The market town of Morpeth had, by the end of March, raised the sum of £2,448; an average of over £7 3s per person resident in the town (over £123,000 today and over £350 per person). Local groups had been key to raising such funds with organisations and clubs holding regular events such as the concert held in March by the men and women of the Morpeth Carol

Society which raised the sum of £17 (almost £860 today). The local Rotary Club had also been very active in holding whist and bridge drives and had plans to augment the £40 (over £2,000) already raised for a fund to provide comforts for men and women from Morpeth who were serving, by holding a free gift sale at the Borough Hall Salesrooms.

As we have seen, the people of south-east Northumberland were not only contributing by raising money but also, in the case of many local women, by providing knitted garments for the war effort. The Central Hospital Supply Service (CHSS) provided materials and equipment to the many voluntary local hospital supply depots around the country with one being the Morpeth Hospital Supply Depot (MHSD) which was run by Mrs Speke (chairwoman) and Mrs Boden (honorary secretary) of the Castle, Morpeth, who was also deputy leader of the local WVS (with which the MHSD was closely linked). In the final fortnight of March, the volunteers of the MHSD had knitted and dispatched fifty pairs of socks, twenty-two pairs of operating stockings, eleven pairs of minesweepers' gloves and forty-two miscellaneous knitted garments to three local hospitals (the two at Stannington and St George's at Morpeth) and four ARP posts. The MHSD had also overseen the dispersal of almost 550 bandages of various types, 202 field dressings, 200 swabs, 20 pairs of pyjamas, 5 pneumonia jackets, 4 dressing gowns, 4 bed-covers, 6 bed jackets, 12 padded splints, 36 night-gowns, 17 day shirts and 6 'helpless case' shirts to the hospitals and ARP posts.[28] In addition to this contribution the MHSD had also supplied the Local Defence Volunteers with 150 much-needed fixed dressings in cases.

The campaign to stop shipping supplies on the east coast had a serious impact upon the north-east with ports such as Blyth being seriously affected at times by enemy attack and through witnessing the losses in shipping. On the night of 1/2 May, enemy aircraft lay mines in a broad stretch of sea from Berwick to Grimsby, while several determined attacks were made on shipping on the river Blyth. So serious was the mine laying off Blyth that the river was closed to all traffic for a period until minesweepers could clear the field off the mouth of the river. The raid caused concern in Blyth as the public believed that for an important east coast port the town had woefully insufficient anti-aircraft defences. As a result of the public consternation a deputation from Blyth Town Council visited Westminster to urge the relevant ministries to increase the levels of protection afforded the town. This deputation met various officials on 9 May, including Sir Edward Grigg (the newly appointed Under Secretary of State for War), and reported back the following week that talks had been constructive and promises had been made to increase the anti-air protection around the port and town.[29]

Although for security reasons the mayor was unable to say exactly what precautions would be put in place at Blyth he was keen to assure the local public that the delegation had been effective. He was also eager to thank local

MP, R.J. Taylor, and the Deputy Commissioner for the Northern Region, Jack Lawson, MP, for arranging the deputation and the appointment with Sir Edward.

Given that the port at Blyth was home to HMS *Elfin*, an important submarine base, it is somewhat surprising that it was not better protected but part of the greater protection was visible quite quickly as the First World War-era battery at Blyth was upgraded and also received an additional observation post and protection from aerial attack.

Added to the risks of enemy bombing was the danger of having damaged RAF aircraft crash on civilian properties. In the early hours of 6 June, three civilians were killed when a Bristol Beaufort of Coastal Command crashed onto their home at 77 Fifth Row, Ashington: two of the crew were also killed. The civilians were all members of the Cox family: Henry (52) and Eleanor (49) were killed immediately, while the couple's daughter Gladys Audrey (18) died in hospital a few hours later. A son, William (16) survived the dreadful accident.[30] The Beaufort I (L9797 OA-F) of 22 Squadron was returning from a raid on Ghent where it had been hit by flak. While over Northumberland the pilot was blinded by searchlights and in trying to evade the resulting glare hit barrage balloon cables which caused an engine to fail and the aircraft to vibrate severely before becoming uncontrollable. The pilot, Pilot Officer Westlake, gave the order to bail out but only he and his navigator (Sergeant S.G. Twitchen) were able to do so successfully. The remaining two crewmen (wireless operator and air gunner) were Sergeant Llewellyn Edwin Thomas Harris (20) and Sergeant Patrick O'Flaherty (23): both airmen were buried in Britain, Harris in Portsmouth and O'Flaherty, who was an Irishman from County Mayo, at Chevington in Northumberland.

The funeral of the three civilians was held on 10 June and such was the sympathy in Ashington that thousands turned out to line the half-mile route of the cortege from Mr Cox's brother's house to the cemetery. With police lining the route a hush descended as soon as the coffins were brought into sight. The cortege itself was the largest the district had ever seen with over 300 people taking part including 50 members of the ARP services (men and women) led by Councillor J.T. Barrass and Mr A. Whitcombe. The rest of the cortege consisted largely of friends and family of Mr and Mrs Cox and young friends of their daughter. In front of the first hearse were two wreaths carried by Mrs Eastlake and Mrs Hope, while the coffin of Gladys was accompanied by two wreaths carried by two particularly close friends of hers.

Before passing into the churchyard the flower-draped coffins passed between a guard of honour made up of ARP workers. With the church full to capacity (including the presence of local members of parliament, representative of the Labour Party, various social clubs and the pigeon club to which Mr Cox had belonged) and hundreds gathered in the churchyard, a simple but very moving ceremony took place before the deceased were buried. The gravesides were marked by a huge number of wreaths including from the RAF and from West End Social Club. Giving some idea of the high esteem in which the late Mr Cox was held there were also wreaths from various collieries, social associations and the local ARP Wardens' posts. Mrs Cox and their daughter also had a large collection of wreaths from family and friends with female neighbours of Mrs Cox having a collection to buy a wreath and inscribed vase, while workmates of William also sent a wreath. For many hours after the service local people visited the churchyard to pay their respects at the graves. The surviving son, William, was not present as his injuries were so severe that, at the time of the funeral, he was still in hospital and was unaware of the loss of his family.

One of the effects of the increasing war on the sea was a rapid surge in the shortage of foodstuffs. With councils and members of the public being urged to grow ever-increasing amounts of their own food Blyth Town Council met to discuss the disused site at North Farm. In pre-war years this was to be built up as a housing estate but these plans had fallen through because of the war and Councillor J.R. Ferrell urged the council to take over the land for the growing of potatoes. Somewhat surprisingly he was opposed in this by the chair of the Housing Committee, Alderman Rafferty, who said that the land had been recommended for use as grazing for horses and that was all that could be done with it. This ludicrous stance was quickly opposed by Councillor Ferrell who stated that the council could surely take over the land for the duration and reminded the council that in pre-war years this patch of and had previously been used to grow potatoes and, indeed, had 'produced some of the best potatoes in the north'.

The debate highlighted two opposing attitudes on the council with one group recognising that land for food production would be increasingly vital during the war while others were more complacent and still focused on a seemingly pre-war mentality that land was already available. Heading this second group was Alderman J.H.M. Twaddle who said that if they went down this path then people would begin to set up allotments 'in the middle of housing estates and then people would object'. Councillor Ferrell immediately said that he was not envisaging letting members of the public set up allotments wherever they wished but for the council to organise the matter. He was backed up by Councillor Barron who reminded his colleagues that the merchant fleet of Britain would have an immense task ahead of it and that if they could, as a corporation, save space by growing as much produce at home as possible then that would only benefit the war effort. Alderman Twaddle countered by saying that he would oppose any new committee being formed which had plenary powers over the use of land because next would be the ploughing up of the cricket pitch, golf course and football field. Alderman Walton then said that the Allotments Committee already had plenary powers over some land but was interrupted by Councillor Mordue who said that the land in question had always been used as grazing and that the local farmer had not requested it to be ploughed up and furthermore that the land had sewers and roads partially built which would make it difficult. Councillor Ferrell then put forward an amendment which asked for a committee to be set up to look at local vacant plots but that final decisions would be left to the council as a whole. He concluded by saying that he wanted 'this thing done at once. We could get potatoes and greens and anything useful for food if we get on with it. The land will be of no use for building until the war is over'.[31]

The local branches of the WI performed a magnificent job in raising funds, helping the displaced, feeding war workers and providing advice to housewives affected by wartime shortages. Problems of food supplies were always at the forefront and the lecture given to the Hepscott branch by Miss Tully of Bedlington was typical. The subject was wartime cookery and Miss Tully went into great detail during her lecture and demonstration of how it was possible to provide a balanced and varied diet without resorting to the use of the meat ration.

The closures of schools and the fact that many were quickly taken over for war purposes such as first aid posts and emergency feeding stations meant that some areas experienced a shortage of available space when many of the initial wartime evacuees returned. Blyth Town Council was forced to request the closure of the first aid post at New Delaval School as the facilities were desperately needed for educational purposes.

Although the closure of schools had caused an increase in juvenile crime and concerns were being expressed over the moral rectitude of young people in the area, one event in June highlighted the courage and self-sacrifice of some youngsters. While walking along the River Blyth, young Stakeford lad Frederick A. Redpath (16) witnessed a young boy slip off the quayside into the river. It became clear that the youngster, Stephen Allan Armstrong, could not swim and was in imminent danger of drowning and Redpath had no hesitation in taking off his greatcoat and jumping in after the lad, despite the fact that the river was 200yds wide, 30ft deep and a large tide was running. When he reached Armstrong, however, the young lad grabbed him a drowning man's embrace which threatened to pull the rescuer under the surface and there could have been a disaster if a passing Belgian seaman hadn't seen the struggle and jumped in to assist. Together the two got the youngster ashore thus saving his life. Awarding a Royal Humane Society Vellum Certificate Alderman A.McHugh said that Redpath had 'exhibited the true characteristics of the Britisher' and 'saw no danger'.[32]

First aid posts were scattered throughout the communities of south-east Northumberland and were another firm reminder of expectations in the event of raiding. As we have seen, many of them were located in schools or in disused council buildings and many also served as the bases of the first aid parties who would respond to the scene of an incident at the request of the local control centre. The demand for drivers was high in these first aid parties, which provided ambulances in order to be able to respond to incidents in neighbouring areas. A typical example, the Whitley Bay area maintained two first aid posts. These two posts, at the Garden Café and at West Monkseaton High School, were home to nine first aid parties and eleven ambulances, which were stationed at these locations or in nearby premises. Manned for twenty-four hours a day, seven days a week, placing great strain upon the volunteers the staff also had to quickly adjust to witnessing sights that few would have seen before. As they responded to incidents immediately during raids they also placed themselves at great risk: inevitably this led to some casualties.

The possibility of invasion and/or raids also led to a raft of new defence regulations, which many fell foul of through ignorance or mischance. Amongst these was the command that all unattended motor vehicles should be disabled so as to render them useless to invaders or spies. Morpeth magistrates were quick to warn people to lock their cars, wind up windows and remove ignition keys when they left the vehicle. The first such case to come before them resulted in a substantial fine of 10s for Andrew Hall Marshall (23), a farmer from North Charlton, who had left his vehicle unattended with the engine running on Newgate Street on 22 June. Motoring offences continued to be a source of concern with magistrates beginning to crack down on infringements of the blackout after having given repeated warnings. Two Morpeth residents, Margaret Elizabeth Wensley of 2 Lady's Walk and John Thomas Wightman (48) of 27 Wellway, were both fined 15s apiece for such offences. Other motoring offences to be heard in June included a case of driving without a licence and one of driving without due care and attention. This case seems to have been rather a stern interpretation of the law as it involved a purely accidental collision at a junction at Bullers Green between two cars. The driver blamed for the collision was a 39-year-old engineer from Forest Hall but eyewitness testimony claimed that the driver's vision had been obscured by a broken-down hand cart and his solicitor argued that his client was, at the most, guilty only of an error of judgement. However, the Forest Hall man was fined 10s with £1 costs.

Even though the vast majority of residents of south-east Northumberland were fully behind the war effort at this critical time there were always some who were more than willing to exploit the wartime situation in order to increase profit. In May, Blyth Town Council discussed an unnamed landlord in the town who had printed a large number of documents stating that he would in the future be charging all those who fell into rent arrears an extra penny per shilling per week throughout the war. The council calculated that this was an effective increase in interest of over 433 per cent and declared that such actions broke 'the law entirely'. The council were unanimous in voicing their approbation over this action and, while urging the landlord to withdraw his policy, threatened legal action advising all those affected to contact the police or local courts.

With the growing shortages it was no surprise that the public became easily angered by those who sought to sell food or drink which was not of the expected quality. A particular problem throughout the war was the watering down of milk. On 15 May, the magistrates at Morpeth heard three such cases and all those charged were found guilty, with fines ranging from 5s to £5 3s. The largest case was that of Pegswood farmer Hector Brewis. Mr Brewis, of North Farm, was a well-known and respected local farmer whose milk had been sold locally by a number of employees for over 25 years. One of these sellers, George Riddell, sold a pint of milk to the local food and drinks inspector, Thomas Wight, who sent the milk away to be tested with the result that it was found to contain approximately 17 per cent added water. When questioned by the police, Mr Brewis stated that he had not been in the dairy for ten days or so and that his employees ran the majority of the operation. He also stated that he prided himself in the quality of his milk and that he trusted the people who worked for him. His dairy workers stated that they had not added water and the only explanation they could offer was that water used to scald the utensils had not been completely emptied and milk had then been poured into the container. The magistrates, largely due to Mr Brewis' reputation, agreed that there had been no intent and that the incident had occurred because of 'negligence on the part of an assistant' and, after fining Mr Brewis heavily, stated that they had 'every confidence in Mr Brewis'.[33] The other cases were of a more minor nature and involved the sale of milk, by Mrs Catherine Alice Purvis, from a shop in the Market Place, Morpeth, and the remaining case was from further north in the county at Red Row.

As we have seen previously, suspicion surrounding foreigners was rampant from the beginning of the war and this wariness extended beyond those of German or Italian descent to include even those of allied nations and those whose countries had been conquered by the Nazis. This latter group included servicemen in all branches of the forces but the doubts were particularly keen surrounding those who were employed as merchant sailors. In Blyth thirteen such men (nine Dutch, three Danes and a Norwegian) found themselves before the magistrates in May after being accused of missing curfew. All were found guilty and fined.

The Dutch nationals, all from one ship, were found in a public house at 9.40 pm by a local police officer despite their papers clearly stating that they could only be ashore between 6.00 am and 8.00 pm. The officer made several requests for the men, including the master of the ship, to return to their vessel but they refused to do so and were subsequently arrested. Through an interpreter one of the Dutchmen said that the incident was the result of confusion and pleaded for leniency saying 'we have got no home'. Clearly there were problems of interpretation as one of the officers was unable to understand the interpreter provided and it was fortunate that one of the magistrates, Mrs Alderson, spoke fluent Dutch and, through her, the officer said that while he understood the regulations he believed that they were unfair when 'his country was now fighting the enemy'. Despite this the magistrates found all of the men guilty and fined them the sum of £1 1s apiece.[34]

One of the Danish sailors had been found wandering around Blyth in the early hours and it was established that the ship he had last been registered on had sailed four days previously. In mitigation the sailor admitted that he had been paid off at South Shields and had made his way to Blyth as he had a friend there but, rather bizarrely given that he must have travelled through or past Newcastle, argued that he was intending to make his way to the Scandinavian Sailors' Home at Newcastle (this was used as a base for Scandinavian sailors during the war and was very well supported). Members of the bench were clearly unimpressed and fined the man the same as his Dutch colleagues.

As a result of the Nazi conquest of France and the Low Countries the possibility of invasion became foremost in the minds of most and to many it seemed clear that a great air battle would be the precursor to any attempt. To this end the government urged people to give up their aluminium kitchen utensils which, they were told, would be used to produce more aircraft. In Morpeth, the collection was quickly organised and supplies began to be gather and sorted by ARP wardens at the town hall. Townspeople were informed by the press of the desperate need and told that Britain's main pre-war supplier had been France. Households were asked to give generously of 'pots, pans, steamers, knives, forks, teapots, toys, lamps, etc.' and assured that if they could not get to the town hall collection could be arranged.[35]

As the Phoney War came to a sudden end and the blitzkrieg rolled over France the people of south-east Northumberland knew that many of their loved ones would be placed in extreme danger. One of the effects of the invasion of France was the removal of the restrictions which prevented the aircraft of Bomber Command from bombing targets inside Germany. On the night of 11 May, just two days after the beginning of the blitzkrieg, a small force of bombers was dispatched to bomb the town of Monchengladbach: an important railway hub. Results were poor and three aircraft were lost. The single Armstrong-Whitworth Whitley which was lost contained Sergeant Thomas Todd Atchison (23) of 8 Burdon Terrace, Bedlington. Sergeant Atchison was the Observer in the 77 Squadron crew of Flying Officer T.H. Parrott and was killed along with three other crewmen.[36] Sergeant Atchison was unfortunate to be aboard the first British bomber to crash within Germany while carrying out a bombing mission on a German town.

The press coverage of the Battle of Britain, combined with radio broadcasts regarding the efforts of Bomber Command, led to an ever greater appreciation for the efforts of the men of the RAF and, with several bases located in the county, the people of Northumberland were eager to help in any way possible. We have already seen how charitable the people of the area could be in giving aid to the services but many went further in agreeing to become a 'home away from home' for members of the RAF. Lord Allendale had appealed for Northumbrians to act as hosts for those airmen based in the county and the people of south-east Northumberland had responded enthusiastically. The reaction was so great that the press was able to report in September that 'every officer and man stationed in Northumberland will now have an opportunity for occasional periods of rest in congenial and homely surroundings'.[37] Feeding arrangements were handled by the commanding officer of the various airmen involved arranging for ration cards being sent to the hosts in advance of arrival. Although this scheme was good for the morale of the airmen concerned and many friendships developed it could also lead to grief when an adopted airman was killed or injured.

One of the Northumbrian pilots taking part in the hectic fighting over France was Flight Lieutenant John Sample who was serving as a B Flight commander with 607 (County of Durham) Squadron. John was a Morpeth man and had worked for his uncle as a land agent in his hometown before the war. The fighting was very intense with many pilots flying five or six sorties every day following the German invasion in May. Because of losses Flight Lieutenant Sample often found himself acting as the commanding officer of the squadron. On the first day of the offensive, Sample shared in the shooting down of two German bombers before he was himself shot down by defensive fire and forced to bail out of his Hurricane. After just two weeks in action, 607 Squadron was forced to return to Britain as a result of losses.

For Sample, however, the campaign was already over. After bailing out he had severely sprained both ankles. His injuries meant that he did not fly again during the Battle of France and upon recovery he was forced to wear slippers even when flying. Back in England he was given command of 504 (County of Nottingham) Squadron in Scotland. In June, he was awarded the DFC for his inspirational actions while in France and in September he was promoted to Squadron Leader before moving his squadron from Scotland to Hendon to take part in the final stages of the Battle of Britain. Fighting throughout this period, Sample claimed a further four enemy bombers either destroyed or damaged and, after the battle, led his squadron on fighter sweeps over France.

Amongst those who were posted missing during the chaos of the fighting in the blitzkrieg and the fighting retreat to Dunkirk was a well-known Northumbrian religious figure. The Reverend Simeon E. Cole had been the leader of Ashington Mission for several years before the war and was also well-known for his work in Newcastle. Upon the outbreak of war, the Reverend Cole had been appointed as a chaplain to the British Expeditionary Force. Thankfully, it was revealed in September that the Reverend had not been killed as was feared and had in fact been taken prisoner near Dunkirk.

The evacuation of the BEF from the beaches of Dunkirk was, of course, a huge talking point in south-east Northumberland and much praise was attached to those local men who had been in action during the withdrawal and evacuation. Given that the Northumberland Fusiliers had been present and played a substantial role it is hardly surprising that several local and locally known officers came in for praise. Amongst them was Major (temporary Lieutenant Colonel) Lechmere Cay Thomas who had led the 9th Northumberland Fusiliers and two attached cavalry regiments in a counter-attack near Hazenbrouck. Thomas was subsequently awarded the DSO for his actions to go along with the MC and the OBE which he already held.[38] Other officers with local connections to be mentioned favourably included: Captain E.B.L. Hart;[39] Lieutenant Dankin; Lieutenant J.H. Sanderson; Lieutenant Bastable; Lieutenant F. Walton; Lieutenant C. Elliott; and Lieutenant R. Simpson.

The evacuation of shattered RAF squadrons was also proceeding and although some of the aircrew were fortunate enough to be able to fly back to Britain, many more and all ground personnel were faced with the arduous retreat (either to Dunkirk or to other French ports) along with their comrades in the army. Many British nationals and RAF ground crew could not reach Dunkirk in time to be evacuate and a fortnight later an attempt was made to lift them from the port of St Nazaire. For the men of 73 Squadron there was further tragedy on 17 June when the HMT *Lancastria* was sunk off the coast of St Nazaire and forty of the squadron's ground personnel were lost. These included Leading Aircraftman George William Bassam (30) of Newsham.[40]

The sinking of the *'Lancastria'* also claimed the life of 35-year-old Private Michael Gorman of 73rd Company, Auxiliary Military Pioneer Corps. Private Gorman was from Ashington where he lived at 70 Ariel Terrace and his body was washed up in France several months later and, after being identified, he was buried, along with many who were lost aboard the troopship, at Pornic War Cemetery.

As the south of the country observed the ongoing Battle of Britain with bated breath, Morpeth lost another son who was to die far from the scene of this battle. Pilot Officer William Appleby was serving as a Wireless Operator/Air Gunner in 269 Squadron based at Wick in the far north of Scotland. The Squadron flew Hudson I aircraft on anti-shipping strikes and maritime patrols across the North Sea. This was a very dangerous role and the squadron suffered numerous casualties. However, it was not down to enemy action that

William lost his life but a terrible and, in wartime, all too common flying accident. In the early hours of 23 July, William was part of the crew of Flight Lieutenant Charles D.W. Price and was setting out on a typical convoy escort of the period. While taking off, the Hudson in which they were flying (P5152, coded UA-J) was in collision with a Hurricane of 3 Squadron. The Hudson bomber crashed and caught fire before exploding when its bomb load blew up; the four-man crew, including Pilot Officer Appleby, were all killed.[41] The Hurricane pilot, Flight Lieutenant D.L. Bisgood, was badly injured when his aircraft also crashed but he recovered and returned to duty, winning the DFC and surviving the war.[42]

William had been educated at Morpeth Grammar School before taking employment with Newcastle-on-Tyne Electrical Supply Company's head office at Newcastle. During this period William also worked as a Sunday School teacher at St James', Morpeth. Five years later, in September 1935, he joined the RAF and became a qualified wireless operator, air gunner (he graduated from a special advanced gunnery course at one point) and observer. An experienced and very able wireless operator William was commissioned in January 1940 and posted to 269 Squadron as Signals Officer (a role of some responsibility). While posted in Scotland William had met a Fife woman, Paula Isobel, and fallen in love. The two had married on 1 June 1940; just over seven weeks before he so tragically lost his life.

The body of 26-year-old Pilot Officer Appleby, a married man, was brought back to his home town and he was buried with military honours in the churchyard at Morpeth on 27 July. William had been very popular in Morpeth and the funeral was very well attended: included amongst the congregation were large numbers of young people who had known William. The service was said to be very impressive and was largely conducted by the Rector (Canon F. Baker) who was also senior chaplain to the forces. A number of representatives from the RAF were present and two of the deceased's favourite hymns were sung ('He Who Would Valiant Be' and 'The Day Thou Gavest, Lord, Is Ended'). The RAF contingent acted as pall-bearers, led by Pilot Officer L.B. Clough (also present from the Air Defence Corps Cadets were Flight Lieutenant R.S. Tegner, Flight Lieutenant E.E. Fail, two Corporals and several cadets along with Mr Thomas Matheson of the RAFVR) and saluted the coffin as it was lowered into the grave.

We have already seen how small air raids in June had caused little or no damage but had significantly heightened the awareness of both the authorities and the civilian population. Throughout this period there were several further probing attacks of a minor nature made under cover of darkness before the Luftwaffe attempted a major daytime raid on the north-east. At the beginning of August, another minor raid resulted in bombs being scattered over Fisher Lane Road End near Cramlington, where a house was set on fire, and at Seven Mile House Farm.

Of course, not all raids were free of injury. Two days after the above raid, another raid led to widespread damage in the Morpeth and Stannington area. During the raid, two parachute mines detonated near Stannington Sanatorium killing several cattle in nearby fields but also causing substantial damage to the sanatorium which was being used to house 300 children (thankfully none were seriously injured) and shattering windows across a wide area including in Morpeth. The flying shards of glass caused injuries to several people while the damage to the sanatorium was estimated at £1,000 (approximately £50,500 today). Many bombs went astray and fell in south-east Northumberland where several lambs were killed, but once again little damage was caused highlighting the difficulties faced by the Luftwaffe in bombing at night over an area with a sparse and widely scattered population. Bombs fell in at least six separate locations in the area with the most serious incidents being the death of the lambs mentioned above when HE bombs were dropped at Wintrick Farm, East Thirston, and when a bomb failed to explode (usually coded as a UXB) in a field north of the Belsay to Whalton road, necessitating the roads closure until the bomb could be attended to.

Obviously, such incidents, even when they caused little or no damage or casualties, increased the strain on both the authorities and the civilian population. This, combined with the fear of invasion by parachute landed forces, led to an incident on 14 August when several rather panicked reports were received of parachutes being dropped at Cresswell Farm as well as at Whittingham further north (there were also reports of parachutes being found in the Leeds area on this day) but searches found nothing and the timing of the reports matched with that of a captured German aircraft being flown over the area en route to the south of England for study.

The bitter campaign to maintain Britain's seaborne supplies took a heavy toll of men from south-east Northumberland, especially from coastal communities such as Blyth. At the end of July, Ethel Maud Jones of 39 Hunter Avenue, Blyth, received the news that her husband, Third Engineer Officer John Horace Jones (30), had been lost at sea through enemy action. Third Engineer Officer Jones was aboard the SS *Sheaf Mead* of the Newcastle-based W.A. Souter & Co. Ltd off the coast of Portugal. Shortly before 4 pm on 27 May the unescorted steam merchant of 5,008 tons was struck in the stern by a single torpedo from the U-37. The vessel sank, capsizing after a boiler explosion. Thirty-two crewmen were lost with only five surviving.

With the extensive number of mining communities in the area the culture of the colliery workers was very deeply ingrained. One way in which the mining community helped its own was in a number of miners' welfare scholarships which were available. In early May, a Bedlington schoolgirl, Kathleen M. Dawson, a pupil at Bedlington Secondary School was one of the lucky ones to be awarded such a scholarship.

Just days after this the area received a morale boost when it was announced that a former Blyth man, Lieutenant Richard Been Stannard (38), had been awarded the VC for his courageous actions at Namsos, Norway. Lieutenant Stannard, RNR, was the skipper of HMT *Arab*, a minesweeping trawler. During the Norway campaign he had, along with two of his men, fought a fire on the wharf at Namsos which was threatening a store of thousands of hand grenades. After this he survived numerous air attacks and established an armed camp of trawlermen under the cliffs so that they could obtain some rest when off duty. When leaving the fjord the ship was attacked by another German bomber which ordered him to surrender or be sunk. Lieutenant Stannard instead shot down the bomber before proceeding.

Kathleen M. Dawson of Bedlington. (The Journal)

Throughout five days Lieutenant Stannard and HMT *Arab* withstood thirty-one bombing attacks while the rest camp was repeatedly attacked but it was so well prepared that only one man was wounded during this time. Lieutenant Stannard had been born in Blyth but when his father (captain of a ship) was lost at sea his mother relocated the family to southern England: the Lieutenant maintained contact with many childhood friends and acquaintances. Before the war he had been the captain for the Dominion Line.

On 15 August, the north-east came under attack from the only massed raid that took place over the area during the Battle of Britain. The Luftwaffe, believing that all of Fighter Command's front line squadrons were in the south of the country and that the north was practically undefended, launched a force from the Norway-based Luftflotte 5 to stretch the defences while simultaneously attacking the south.

The attacks on the south came first. These largely concentrated on airfields and were designed to keep the attention of Fighter Command focused firmly on the south of England. However, fate played a role and, unbeknown to the Luftwaffe, the radar operators of 13 Group were on full alert, monitoring for possible attacks on a large convoy expected to sail from Hull. Just after midday they detected a raid which at first was believed to be heading for Edinburgh. As it became clear that the raid was stronger than at first believed and was altering course southwards the decision was taken to scramble the Spitfires of 72 Squadron from Acklington with orders to head for the Farne Islands while 79 Squadron's Hurricanes were placed on standby. Subsequently the Hurricanes of 605 and 607 Squadrons were also placed on standby.

As the radar picture became clearer it was obvious that this was a serious raid. The more northerly of the two German formations was in fact a diversion intended to draw off fighters and consisted of HE 115 seaplanes which had orders to turn back before reaching the coast. Unfortunately any chance of the deception working was destroyed as the lead navigator of the actual bombing force, which consisted of 72 HE 111s led by Oberstleutnant Fuchs, had made an error and was too far north meaning that the radar return seen by 13 Group seemed to be one very large raid and Air Vice-Marshal (AVM) Saul reacted appropriately. The operators were also aware of a more southerly and smaller plot which was in fact the escort which had been assigned to Fuchs' formation. This escort consisted of twenty-one long range ME 110s loaded with extra fuel and led by their commander, Werner Restemeyer. Upon sighting the two formations attempting to link up, 72 Squadron reported a raid of 100 plus enemy aircraft with the result that three further squadrons were scrambled (41, 607, which was ordered to patrol Tyneside, and 79).

Meanwhile, 72 Squadron found itself in an ideal position to attack, being some 4,000ft higher than the German formations. Squadron Leader Edward (Ted) Graham was at first slightly nonplussed as to what action was best and when asked by another pilot if he had seen the Germans stammered the now infamous reply, 'Of course I've seen the b-b-b-bastards, I'm t-t-t-trying to work out what to do,' before leading his squadron down in a flank attack on the escorts which took them through into the bomber formation below.[43] Two ME 110s were immediately shot down, including Restemeyer's which blew up dramatically when bullets hit the fuel tank, and the escorts scattered in confusion. The subsequent attack on the bombers also resulted in the formation losing coherency and many of the Heinkels jettisoned their bombs in panic. Five minutes later RAF reinforcements arrived and very quickly a further eight HE 111s and six more ME 110s were shot down for only two damaged Hurricanes (both from 605 Squadron) and one wounded pilot.

AVM Richard E. Saul CB DFC had handled his forces in an exemplary manner and they, along with the Tyne anti-aircraft defences, had turned aside a major Luftwaffe attack for no serious loss to themselves and with little or no damage done on the ground. The action was witnessed by few people directly although many Northumbrians in coastal towns and villages saw aircraft and heard the combats, and at Amble four German airmen were brought ashore after their HE 111 had been shot down off Druridge Bay. The actions of the RAF aircrew and the tactics of AVM Saul resulted in the Luftwaffe giving up any hope of launching further heavy daylight raids on Northumberland and Tyneside.[44]

The local press reported the event with a substantial dose of hyperbole claiming that the enemy force had consisted of over 300 aircraft and that their 'wings darkened the sky over the North Sea'. They claimed that the RAF had managed to shoot down '75 bombers in as many minutes without loss to themselves'.[45]

At the end of August, the Luftwaffe resumed night operations against the area and despite the primary target usually being Tyneside bombs continued to fall haphazardly over south-east Northumberland. On 24/25 August, Broomhill Colliery Farm was hit by several HE bombs which caused the death of twenty-seven sheep (it is likely the target was the barracks at RAF Acklington some 200 yards away). The randomness of such bombing was explained by aircraft becoming lost after the long dark crossing over the North Sea and jettisoning their bombs on targets of opportunity or even simply jettisoning. On this night, for example, a single HE bomb was recorded as having fallen at Seaton Sluice doing little damage.

Keen to keep up the pressure the Luftwaffe tried again the next night and once again bombs seem to have been scattered widely, with Broomhill hit again along with Hepscott, Shiremoor and New York. The most serious of these incidents was the one at Shiremoor when almost twenty bombs were dropped falling roughly north to south over the area. Ten of the bombs seem to have been aimed at the LNER line which ran through the village. One of these destroyed two houses in Grange Avenue (no's 2 and 4) while three bombs fell near to the modern school, two in house gardens in Whitley Row and one across from 4 James Avenue. As a result of these incidents two people received slight injuries and a woman was trapped in one of the demolished properties but was later rescued by the ARP services.

The series of raids continued the same night with yet more bombs hitting communities including Longhirst, Ellington, Ashington, Cambois, Seaton Delaval and Earsdon. At least one aircraft appeared to be lost around 10.30 pm as flares were seen descending in the Longhirst area and were followed by over 100 incendiaries at Jordan's Farm, Longhirst, and in the Ellington area. At Morpeth a bomb fell but failed to explode at The Rectory, causing some anxiety and disruption for the residents. A feature of this raid was the use of incendiary oil bombs which were dropped at Bates Cottages, North Linton and Ashington. Although fires were caused these were quickly brought under control and there were no casualties recorded. However, the water supply in several areas was cut by explosive bombs or by UXBs. The following night another smaller raid was made but the majority of bombs fell further south, in County Durham, with Whitley Bay, which was attacked by several aircraft, being the only community in south-east Northumberland to suffer. One of the attacking aircraft was shot down, crashing at Hartley.

Not all casualties resulted from enemy action. Training continued to take a deadly toll throughout the period. In September, a telegram arrived at the Newbiggin-by-the-Sea home of the parents of Pilot Officer Harry Reed Stothard (23) informing them that their eldest son had been killed in a flying accident while serving at the training base at RAF Lossiemouth. The base at this period was being used by Bomber Command's 20 Operational Training Unit (OTU). Pilot Officer Stothard was an experienced pilot and before obtaining his RAF commission he was a member of the Newcastle Aero Club.

Of course not all the casualties to men from the area occurred in Europe: fighting in the deserts of North Africa also took their toll. On 28 July, Flight Lieutenant Ian Cheesman Swann of 30 Squadron, RAF, lost his life while flying on a bomber escort mission over Libya. Swann was a native of Throckley and was aged just 21 when he was killed. The unfortunate pilot is buried at Knightsbridge War Cemetery, Acroma, Libya.

Casualties continued to occur outside of the men of Fighter Command and their battle over the British mainland as the other RAF commands, especially Bomber Command and Coastal Command, continued in action against the Germans. On 14 October, Ashington man Sergeant John Jackson Wilks (27) lost his life while flying in a Coastal Command Lockheed Hudson of 233 Squadron. Taking off from their base at RAF Leuchars just after 5.00 am, tasked for a reconnaissance of the Norwegian coast in Hudson I (T9343 ZS-Z) nothing further was heard and the four-man crew was declared missing. It emerged that the Hudson had been shot down by the Messerschmitt ME109 of future ace German pilot Oberleutnant Horst Carganico with the death of all four crewmen, including the highly experienced pilot, Flight Lieutenant Rowley and Sergeant Wilks.[46]

The south-east of Northumberland had a fine reputation for producing professional footballers and many of these young men joined up at the outset of the war. On 18 September one of these men, Robert Henry Gordon, died of wounds sustained while serving with 9 Squadron, RAF Bomber Command. Gordon was born at Shankhouse and had played for his local team before being taken onto the books of Huddersfield Town FC, aged just 18, where he was a reserve for the regular wing half and made a total of seven first team appearances, demonstrating great potential according to the local press.[47]

In September, many local schools held prize-giving ceremonies to honour academic achievement. At Bedlington Station Council School, for example, the prizes were handed out by the wife of the headmaster, Mr R. Bullerwell. Prizes were given out for academic excellence and for contributions to the school. These included the awarding of books to the head boy, Alan Calvert, and head girl, Constance Baldry.

Mrs Bullerwell hands prize books to head boy and head girl of Bedlington Station Council School. (The Journal)

Volunteers played a key part in getting the harvest gathered in with women and schoolchildren playing a leading role. Through late September and early October the focus shifted to the potato harvest and once again women and children made the major contribution. At this stage many farmers in south-east Northumberland were still using traditional techniques including the use of horses and horse-drawn implements despite the fact that this was labour intensive.

As winter approached, the Home Office once more ordered local authorities to impose early closing times upon shopkeepers in order to help enforce the blackout. In Morpeth this caused outrage among local traders as the council informed them that all shops must close at 5.30 pm on weekdays and 6.00 pm on Saturdays. The irate shopkeepers assembled an emergency meeting of the Morpeth Tradesmen's Association to discuss the matter. The chairman, Mr Malcolm Wood, stated that he agreed that the given hours were too early and accused the council of being duplicitous in their claims that Councillor Grey had consulted members of the food trades. As evidence of this Mr Wood, who himself worked in this trade, asserted that he had certainly not been consulted and that if he had he would have immediately have

Potato pickers at Hartford Home Farm, near Bedlington. (The Journal)

convened a meeting of the association to discuss the matter. The association agreed that while they had always had good relations with the council they felt strongly that they should have been consulted and that what was suitable for one trade was not suitable for all. They voted in favour of the following hours: 6.00 pm on Monday, Tuesday and Wednesday; 12.30 pm on Thursday (early closing day); and 7.00 pm on Friday and Saturday. They also agreed to send a delegation (consisting of Mr Wood, Mr Goldstraw (the secretary), Mr P. Lawson and Mr B. Jobson) to discuss the matter with the council.

After lengthy discussions with the authorities, a settlement was reached to put in place a trial period with shops open until 5.30 pm on Monday, Tuesday and Wednesday, 12.30 pm on Thursday and 7.00 pm on Friday and Saturday.

Despite the ongoing conflict and the threat posed to Britain's very survival, the people of south-east Northumberland continued to find time to commemorate the previous World War. Remembrance services were well attended on 11 November with the one at the Congregational Church in Morpeth attracting particular comment for its poignancy. Before the two minutes silence Captain Wilkinson hung a wreath of Flanders poppies beneath the church's memorial and afterwards the following verse was quoted:

> 'O Valiant Hearts, who to your glory came
> Through dust of conflict and through battle flame
> Tranquil you lie, your knightly virtue proved,
> Your memory hallowed in the land you loved.'[48]

For many former pupils of Morpeth Grammar School November brought the sad news that the famous fir tree that for many years had stood at the front of the school had succumbed to the gale that blew through the town on 21 November. Coverage in the local press indicated that the tree held an especial place in the memory of a great many former pupils and entreated the governors to look into the possibility of planting a replacement.

In Ashington the virtues of American and Canadians were extolled to a large gathering of Boy Scouts and other youth associations at the town's Arcade Hall. The speakers were themselves scout troop leaders who had both been decorated for valour as ARP messengers during the blitz (Hugh Bright (Glasgow) and John Bethell (Birkenhead)) and sent on a morale-raising tour of Canada and the USA. The two troop leaders spoke of how enthusiastically they were greeted by large crowds in both countries and how they were asked questions regarding the conduct of the British people during war, rationing and air raids. They also spoke of how many Americans held erroneous beliefs about the British way of life but also of how they had seen huge factories producing war material and had observed large trains full of, presumably, Canadian volunteers.

While some lucky youths had been abroad, the lack of tourists in Britain badly affected some businesses in south-east Northumberland, with the economies of coastal communities being particularly hard hit. Typical of the types of businesses which simply could not cope was that of the confectionary, novelties and tobacco shop of Mrs Cissie Close of Newbiggin. Mrs Close's shop had been open for seventeen years and was popular with residents and visitors but became 'a civilian casualty of the war' with Mrs Close reluctantly leaving and transferring the remaining stock to a nearby shop owned by her husband.[49]

One of the most vexing occurrences in wartime Northumberland was the almost continuous examinations of identity papers by the police. Although necessary for security purposes, at times it seems the authorities could be overly zealous as it was easy, through ignorance, to fall foul of the regulations. At the end of November the case of 18-year-old butcher George Henry Shepherd came before the bench in his home town of Morpeth. Mr Shepherd had been stopped by a police sergeant in New Market, Morpeth, and asked to present his identity papers. Upon examination they revealed a home address in York and Mr Shepherd was asked how long he had been back in Morpeth to which he replied that he had been resident for approximately three months. The sergeant then asked if he had visited the local registration office to notify them of his change of address and after being told he had not he was arrested. At the hearing, Superintendent Scott pressed for harsh justice saying that although this was the first such case to come before the bench at Morpeth he wanted the bench and the press to be aware that it was an offence to fail to report to the local registration office if away from one's registered address for more than seven days. Councillor W.D. Forster-Coull, the chairman, was clearly minded to be more understanding and asked if the offence was perpetrated through mere carelessness and the clerk, Mr H. Graham Barrow, agreed arguing that the age of the accused should be taken into account too. As a result of their deliberations the bench decided to dismiss the case on payment of costs but added, for the benefit of the press, that the case must be taken as a warning to others.

The black market was, of course, active throughout the war and wartime conditions in south-east Northumberland workplaces and in military installations resulted in many opportunities for petty and organised larceny. Members of the armed forces seem to commonly have been involved in such crimes. Typical was the case of Private Richard Woodhouse (27) who was accused of stealing two cartons of cigarettes from the Navy, Army and Air Force Institution store at Winton House, Morpeth. Private Woodhouse was employed at the institute at the time and was caught red-handed in the storeroom by the manager and area manager; he confessed immediately saying 'I am sorry, old man … I am sorry. I am in real trouble. I want money to send home' and adding that he had found the door open and the temptation had proven too great.[50]

The reasons for such crimes varied but, aside from simple greed, often had wartime hardships at their roots. This was no exception and it was revealed during the hearing that Private Woodhouse was a married man with three young children, all of whom were evacuees in Northumberland, and no previous problems with the law. He revealed that his mother and sister were in London and he wished to get some money together to bring them north so that they could live as a family. This was clearly true as Private Woodhouse was a non-smoker and confessed in full to the police immediately he had been apprehended. The bench could not overlook the theft but seem to have been willing to take into account the circumstances and the accused's previous good character and fined him the sum of £1.

Crime continued to be a problem despite, and is some cases because of, the wartime situation. There was an interesting day at Blyth Police Court in mid-December when a hearing coincided with the inauguration of the mayor of the town. The gentleman presiding on the bench was the town's first Mayor, Mr J. Goulding, and, after congratulating the newest incumbent, Alderman W.W. Mather, he invited the new mayor, in line with town custom, to dismiss the first case and a cyclist who had admitted ignoring traffic signs was duly pardoned. The next offender was not so fortunate and local miner Henry Williams (33) was duly sentenced to three months' imprisonment after being found guilty of the theft of 8 stone of potatoes and a bicycle from a shed at Kitty Brewster Farm, in Cowpen.

Elsewhere in south-east Northumberland more respectable events were taking place. The majority of people in the area remained proud of the contributions made by volunteers who served in services such as the Home Guard and ARP. They were also keen to ensure that the sacrifices and victories of previous generations were commemorated during the remembrance period and parades in November and December were commonplace. At Burradon, a large parade including men and women from the British Legion, Home Guard, Auxiliary Fire Service (AFS), ARP and others was accompanied by the local Burradon and Weetslade colliery band. Following the parade, which attracted a substantial crowd, a short service was held at the Burradon War Memorial Cottage.

As the year drew to a close and people began to reflect on what had been possibly the most tumultuous year in British history many turned to the familiar succour of religion for comfort and reassurance. Church attendances were higher than average in the final months of the year and a number of annual rallies were held successfully. In November, these included the Christian Endeavour rally at Annitsford Methodist Church which saw nine churches attending to hear Shiremoor-based speaker W. Nicholson. These included: Dudley, Weetslade Road; Dudley Bethel Methodist; Burradon Bethel; Cramlington Village; Backworth ex-Primitive Methodist; Hartford; Seghill Laycock; Seghill Station Road; and West Moor United Methodist.

Meanwhile, in Seaton Burn the Wesley Guild held its annual weekend rally at Seaton Burn Front Street Methodist Church. Once again a large number of people turned out to hear several speakers including the Reverend A. Wilberforce Hardy.

The men of the light and heavy rescue squads had continued to hone their skills during the year, affecting several successful rescues during and after air raids. One problem to arise, however, was the spread of rumours which seemed to frequently originate from such teams. The rescue workers enjoyed frequent breaks in their working routines and rapidly attracted the reputation for being the leading rumour mongers amongst the ARP services in some areas. ARP canteens were a constant source of rumours and this did on some occasions lead to unfortunate consequences. During one of the 1940 raids on Whitley Bay, a human head was discovered at the scene of a bombing and the relatives of the deceased found out about this discovery via the rumour-mill. This unfortunate and tragic event was investigated and was put down to the gossiping of a team of rescue workers at a local ARP canteen.[51] After this all rescue workers were reminded that their work was confidential and that discussion of incidents outside of work was strictly forbidden.

CHAPTER 3

1941: Defeat on Many Fronts

As the war entered its third year the people of south-east Northumberland reflected upon the averted crises of 1940 and looked with some anxiety towards the new year. So far, news of the war had been bad, with only the 'miracle' of Dunkirk and the Battle of Britain (which was actively portrayed as a victory even though it was a very narrow one) to lighten the mood. The year 1941 would see more reverses, with early victories in Africa against the Italians quickly reversed when Rommel's Afrika Korps became involved in the fighting. Further reverses included the loss of Greece in April and German invasions of Yugoslavia, while in the east Japan was making considerable inroads. The invasion of the Soviet Union in June gave Britain another ally but the Germans made huge advances against the disorganised Russian forces. There was some hope with German and USA relations worsening and culminating in an order, following the sinking of US shipping, that any German vessels found in American waters were to be sunk; at the end of the year Japanese forces launched a devastating attack on the US fleet at Pearl Harbor and Kaneohe Bay, forcing America to finally enter the war. However, the Japanese were in the ascendancy and defeated the British in Malaya before capturing Hong Kong on Christmas Day and threatening the fortress of Singapore; with the British frantically attempting to reinforce the beleaguered forces there in the last days of the year.

The end of January brought the beginning of Blyth's War Weapons Week during which time the town hoped to raise enough money to purchase a minesweeper. To launch the campaign a large parade consisting of service personnel, ARP services personnel and contingents from units such as the ATS took part in very wet conditions.

Concerns over juvenile crime continued throughout the year with the perceived lowering of moral standards amongst youngsters, and especially young women, being regarded with some alarm. The year began with a typical case when Olive Rigg, an 18-year-old domestic servant from Ashington, was sent to a borstal for three years for the crime of having been found sleeping with a soldier in an air raid shelter.

While many south-east Northumbrian families had been relieved that loved ones, posted missing in the confused fighting in France in 1940, had been named as PoWs, the worries certainly did not end there. Conditions within German

Members of the ATS parade through Blyth to launch the town's War Weapons Week. (The Journal)

PoW camps were sometimes extremely unhealthy, and many prisoners succumbed to illness during the years in captivity. Mr and Mrs E. Russell, of Millfield, Bedlington, received notification in February that their son, Fusilier James Russell (20), 7th Battalion, Royal Northumberland Fusiliers, had died in a camp hospital in Poland just two days before he would have celebrated his twenty-first birthday.[52] Like many men from the area who had gone to serve, James was a former miner (he had worked at Bedlington Doctor Pit).

While the area had seen several raids during the previous year, 1941 would prove to be the worst for Northumberland and the North East in terms of frequency of raids. With many bombs falling in open farmland the majority of these raids did little or no damage, but there were some which did considerable damage to property, rendering many people homeless. There were also fatalities.

Fusilier James Russell. (The Journal)

During these raids, the organisation of the ARP services would receive its first real test and lessons would be learned which would be of benefit later. The extremely poor weather of February served to highlight one problem with the Whitley Bay Area Control Room being left isolated after snow brought down telephone lines on the coast. Throughout the year the system's reliance upon telephone communications was repeatedly highlighted as a weakness. In an attempt to combat this, boys between 15 and 18 were recruited, often from the Boy Scouts or Boys' Brigade, to act as volunteer messengers; a highly dangerous role during a raid. Although many were proud of this contribution there were lingering suspicions that many of the boys could not be relied upon to turnout for drills.

The Whitley Bay area experienced problems with some of its voluntary messengers and the service seems to have included a proportion of recalcitrant members. The Whitley Bay ARP Committee reported that 'only a very few were really interested in the service unless there had been an alert ... but certain of the neighbouring areas seemed to have a very efficient Messenger Service and interest was very keen'.[53] Youthful exuberance could also be a problem in the messenger service. On one occasion over a dozen messengers from Whitley Bay grew bored during an early alert and were subsequently found marching along the road in full anti-gas clothing and steel helmets by the police who had been called by concerned residents.

Local wardens had the burden of being first responders to an incident and were usually expected to be the first service to arrive at the scene and so had a crucial role to play. Wardens were often local to their area and often had, or established, relationships with many of the residents. This was usually a positive development, but, where a warden was unpopular, over-stepped his authority or was perceived as being obsessed with his power over the population it could lead to severe difficulties. The local community saw a popular warden as the leader of all air raid precaution policy within his area of influence and often relied upon him (or her) for advice, while others saw them as interfering busybodies.

A large raid on 15/16 February led the editor of a local newspaper to specifically mention how the Home Guard, Police, Air Raid Wardens and builders had all helped hugely in the aftermath. This raid had caused massive damage and casualties in Tynemouth but the mining community of Bedlington had also been hard hit with several rows of houses being demolished although thankfully there had been no fatalities. Incendiaries also took hold in the town and fire damage was caused to several properties including the local Co-op store. Several other nearby communities were also hit. Lynemouth received heavy damage when a parachute mine exploded in the village, wrecking the post office and seven houses, while another sixty houses were so badly damaged that they were rendered uninhabitable. There was a fatality in this attack when 42-year-old Leonora Atthey was killed when her home at 65 Dalton Avenue was destroyed. Other communities to be hit included Ashington, Blyth (where a large number of buildings were damaged), Pegswood, Seaton Delaval and Seaton Sluice.

In addition to those mentioned above, the editor of the paper also praised the charitable efforts of the ordinary people of those communities who despite overcrowding, gladly offered their homes to those who had been unfortunate enough to be bombed out. Concluding in a positive fashion, the author stated that the efforts and attitude of the people involved in these incidents proved that final victory was assured and that because of its character the British people could never 'be brought under the yoke of Nazi domination'.[54]

As a result of this raid questions were asked about several aspects of the civil defence and ARP services in the Bedlington area. The chairman of Morpeth Guardians Committee stated that as he understood it there was no emergency feeding centre in the Bedlington district. It was the women of the WVS who saved the day by quickly organising themselves and, with the aid of the civil defence services, requisitioned a hotel to help feed those who had been made homeless. By 8.00 am they had cooked breakfast for 200 people and were also able to provide a hot meal at noon. Volunteers from the Home Guard and the Boy Scouts also came in for praise, although there were some complaints that some Boy Scouts had used their duties as messengers to go souvenir collecting. Several streets of condemned colliery housing were taken over to provide temporary homes for those who had been bombed out (including one family who had been bombed out in London and then bombed out again at Bedlington).

The concerns over preparedness in the Bedlington district had further repercussions in September when the meeting of the Bedlington Urban Council was dominated by the subject of inadequate provision of shelters for the people of the district. The retired chairman, Councillor Straker, baldly stated that there had been several disappointments during the previous year but the foremost was 'in regard to air raid shelters' and that, despite the best efforts of the council, progress had been far from satisfactory. The new chair, Councillor G.W. Simpson, said that despite the great success of the billeting card system which allowed the ARP services to quickly rehouse those who had been bombed out, there was a great deal of work to be done to safeguard the people of the area.

The surveyor came in for criticism from several councillors when he said that construction of surface air raid shelters was continuing satisfactorily. Councillor Baker said that although he appreciated the difficulties there was an urgent need for the speeding up of the process while Councillor Raffle said that the use of the word 'satisfactorily' was hardly appropriate and Councillor Heslop claimed that the people of West Sleekburn would hardly agree with summation of the surveyor as 'Many people there had no other protection other than that afforded by their houses.' The councillors were particularly critical of two private firms which had been contracted to undertake the erection of the shelters. Councillor Watson did offer some support to the under-fire surveyor and the private contractors when he said that he understood the main problem to be the shortage of necessary supplies. In this he was supported by the chair and by a further statement by the surveyor which agreed that shortages of materials along with labour problems and the difficulties of transportation had all combined to cause the difficulties. Councillor Milburn placed the blame at the feet of the government and said that lessons should have been learned after the Spanish Civil War demonstrated how lethal aerial bombing was to a civilian population. After some further discussion the council agreed that they needed to bring a halt to public criticism and that the only way to do this was to raise the matter with the local MP.[55]

Writing at the end of March, the editor of the Ashington Collieries magazine paid tribute to the efforts of the British people and in particular those of northern England. Motivated by the recent enemy activity which had taken place over Northumberland the editor mentioned how, although the average British person had a happy-go-lucky attitude and was content to go through life grumbling at minor issues and not thinking too much of the future, they always rose magnificently to the occasion when a real crisis occurred. He stated that Dunkirk was just one such example, with the bravery and steadfast courage of the people of London and other towns being another; concluding that this was summed up best in the north country saying: 'sticking it'. He opined that the people of Northumberland could now be added to that list.

Throughout March there were bursts of enemy activity over the county, with raids taking place on six separate nights and alerts on several other occasions. On the night of 3/4 March a raid was made on Tynemouth and Newcastle but several enemy aircraft also dropped bombs in south-east Northumberland. Bombs were recorded at Causey Park, East Sleekburn, Cowpen, Shilvington, Ashington and Morpeth. There was substantial damage done to housing but thankfully no fatalities in the area. Several of the bombs appear to have been dropped after a Luftwaffe crew spotted a light on the ground (the bomb at Sparrow House Farm, Ashington, was dropped close to an aircraft beacon while one at Longhorsley was near a searchlight emplacement) and the authorities began a campaign to remind people of the necessity of maintaining an effective blackout.

Ashington had another taste of enemy bombing on the night of 13/14 March, when there was a raid on the North East which saw bombs dropped at Coneygarth Farm (which was near to an RAF beacon). The bombs caused severe damage to the farm and there were further bombs dropped at Horton

Grange Farm, where a search was carried out for a suspected unexploded bomb but nothing was ever found. For the population of south-east Northumberland and Tyneside it meant another night in the shelters as the alert was sounded at 8.50 pm and the all-clear was not sounded until 4.35 am. Once more lights on the ground attracted bombing with another RAF beacon being bombed at Coneygarth Farm. The RAF and anti-aircraft defences were in action throughout the night and had at least one success when, just after 10.30 pm, a Spitfire of Acklington-based 72 Squadron (piloted by Flight Lieutenant D. Sheen) shot down a Junker JU88 bomber in a sheet of flame into the sea off Amble.[56]

The month had also seen the extension of rationing to include jam, treacle and margarine (8oz per person per month) and a reduction in the amount of meat that was permitted (to just 6oz per week). There had also been the almost routine activity off the coast when German aircraft laid mines and attacked shipping. One such incident, on 17 March, saw His Majesty's Yacht *Mollusc* sunk by Luftwaffe aircraft off Blyth.

Raids continued throughout April with piecemeal attacks and scattered incidents of bombing on many days. On the night of 7/8 April, for example, bombs were dropped on the mining village of Bebside where two bombs left 60ft craters and caused a great deal of damage in Beecher Street while a further two bombs at Bebside Hall brought down telegraph cables and electrical lines. Cramlington was also hit hard on this occasion with bombs, parachute mines and incendiaries all falling on the town and its outskirts. The constant technological battle was given another twist on this occasion when two parachute mines fell but failed to detonate east of Horton Grange. After recovering these mines it was discovered that one was of a previously unknown type and the mine disposal unit took a great deal of interest in it. Many of the bombs which fell on south-east Northumberland during this raid (which was probably intended to target HMS *Manchester* and HMS *Illustrious* which were on the Tyne at the time) appear to have been targeted at collieries or railway lines, with Dudley Colliery being hit by two unexploded bombs and the LNER line being put out of action when a bomb fell on the line near Dudley signal box.

The very next night another raid targeting Tyneside led to damage at Whitley Bay. The alert was sounded shortly before 11.30 pm and people in the far south-east of Northumberland (and across Tyneside) took to their shelters while the ARP services swung into action. The attack was a major one and lasted over five hours and caused severe damage including a fire of over a mile in length along the banks of the Tyne.[57]

Further damage was done at Cowpen on the night of 15/16 April and two nights later incendiary bombs were dropped on Morpeth (at Tommy's Field, Mount Hags Field, St George's Hospital driveway, Thorpe Avenue and East Shield Hill Farm), Cramlington and Dudley. No damage was done by these incendiaries largely thanks to the introduction in March of compulsory fire-watching duties. Highlighting the dangers to civil defence workers two first aid workers from Whitley Bay were killed when their ambulance, which was heading to Tynemouth to give assistance, received a direct hit. The driver, Miss Doris Ewbank (28) of 12 Brundon Avenue, Monkseaton, was a teacher at Backworth Infants' School. In order to avoid damaging morale the news of Miss Ewbank's death during the raid was never widely reported as it was feared that anxious female volunteers (influenced by their families) would withdraw from the ARP scheme. The community, however, was keenly aware of Miss Ewbank's sacrifice and her name is the only civilian one on the Whitley Bay war memorial and plaques were also placed at Panama Gardens and St Mary's Church.[58] The first aid worker killed alongside Miss Ewbank was Edward William Sutton (49), a married man of 147 Cauldwell Lane, Whitley Bay.

Five nights later the Luftwaffe was back when 100 aircraft raided the same area. Once again Whitley Bay suffered badly with fifteen residents being killed, fourteen of them in one street: Ocean View. Many others in the town were injured with seventeen being admitted to emergency hospitals in Tynemouth (one at Preston Hospital and sixteen at Tynemouth Jubilee Hospital). Damage was also caused on this night during a raid on Cowpen, Blyth.

Fatalities in Whitley Bay Raid on Night of 15/16 April 1941.

Name	Age	Location	Notes
George Armstrong	41	21 Ocean View	
Mary Armstrong	41	21 Ocean View	
Annie J. W. Carr	81	12 Ocean View	
Blanche Bertha Carr	71	12 Ocean View	
Robertyne Coltart	82	12 Ocean View	
Annie Grearson	47	17 Mason Avenue	
Elsie Marriam Harrison	39	10 Ocean View	
Thomasina Harrison	67	10 Ocean View	
Catherine Irving	18	16 Ocean View	
Ivy Irving	50	16 Ocean View	
Annie Simpson	56	17 Ocean View	
Marie Simpson	15	17 Ocean View	
Percival Simpson	53	17 Ocean View	ARP Control Centre
William Robert Simpson	14	17 Ocean View	
Susan Ellen Wilson	58	12 Ocean View	

On the night of 25/26 April there was a severe raid on the north-east of England with several fatalities in south-east Northumberland. Bombs on Seghill killed four people while two were killed at Shiremoor and one at Bebside and Blyth.[59] The casualties were as follows:

Name	Age	Place
Thomas Smith	21	1 Station Row, Seghill
Rita Watson	17	4 Station Row, Seghill
Samson Irving	28	Station Row, Seghill
Willliam Morton	56	6 Station Row, Seghill
Isaac Brown	43	7 Catherine Terrace, Blyth
Eric Charlton	10	20 Louisa Street, Shiremoor
Flora Charlton	35	20 Louisa Street, Shiremoor
John Hollon Elliott Norfolk	51	Railway Crossing, Bebside

Damage due to this raid was severe with several bombs falling on Blyth town centre. Alexandra Crescent, Beaumont Street, Bondicar Terrace, Delaval Terrace and Maddison Street all suffered heavy damage as did the town's railway station and the confectionary factory of Redheads. Shelter marshals Jack Furness and George Evans were lauded locally as heroes after they used their own bodies to form a bridge to help occupants of their public shelter to escape after a bomb demolished the entrance. The railway line was temporarily put out of action when bombs destroyed a signal box, lines and rolling stock.

The efforts to provide support to the war effort were continuous and it is to the credit of the people of south-east Northumberland that the majority were so successful in raising funds. In April Bedlingtonshire held its War Weapons Week with a parade of 1½ miles featuring the civil defence forces, the Home Guard, various military units, the Special Constabulary, Boy Scouts, Girl Guides, St John Ambulance and the Auxiliary Fire Service. Included among the parade was motorised equipment of the repair, rescue and decontamination squads along with ambulances from the first aid parties. The parade, headed by three local colliery bands, visited the communities of East Sleekburn, Cambois, West Sleekburn, Stakeford and Scotland Gate. At this last place the parade was inspected by Brigadier General Hanbury Pawle who took the salute as it passed.[60] Other dignitaries took the salute when the parade passed Bedlington Station and Bedlington War Memorial. Donation centres were opened around the district and such was the enthusiasm of the populace that one centre could report having raised £500 in the very first hour of business. The target for the week was to raise £40,000 (over £1,800,000 today) to purchase two bomber aircraft and by the end of the first day £25,000 had already been raised. Other events for the week included various military displays and the exhibition of a shot-down enemy Messerschmitt aircraft.

The week was a great success with the formation of an additional 200 street savings groups and keen participation by all in the district especially amongst the local schools. The committee was delighted to report that their aim of raising £40,000 had not only been reached extremely quickly but that the final tally stood at almost double that figure (over £3,500,000 today) and that the vast majority of donations had come from small investors.

Meanwhile, Ashington and Newbiggin were planning for their own War Weapons Week which was to begin on 3 May. An initial target of £100,000 (comparable to over £4,500,000 today) was set with the first day seeing a large parade in Ashington assembling at the People's Park before marching through the town with the salute being taken by Major General R.C. Money, MC, who was commanding officer of the Northern (County) Division. The Home Guard and civil defence services were already preparing for their part in the parade and the local press reported great anticipation amongst the people of the district. After the parade a public meeting was to be held at the Arcade Hall where speeches would be made by Major General Money and two local MPs (Mr R.J. Taylor, MP, for Morpeth and Mr R. Donald Scott, MP, for Wansbeck). Following this the speakers would head to Newbiggin where a similar parade (this time featuring the Newbiggin Home Guard and civil defence services) would be held, followed by an open air meeting on the moor at the Golf Club.

A large part of the forthcoming campaign was to be the formation of a number of new street savings groups and local head teachers were intensively involved in identifying and encouraging locals to take part. Already over fifty groups had been created in the Newbiggin area, while the small community of North Seaton had also set its own aim of raising £750 (over £34,000 today) from the village. Two touring cinema vans would also encourage people to contribute, while other, more light-hearted, encouragement was also given. Local newspapers ran an interview with the 'flippant philosopher of the Ashington Publicity Committee' who said:

> *[I]f Hitler wins the war you'll be a slave. It means that if you hit Hitler on the nose he will feel it. It means that if you lend a pound to the British Government Hitler will feel it … if you hit Hitler hard enough he won't feel anything, and the only way you can hit him hard enough to knock him out is by lending the Government all you've got to buy weapons to hit him with … Hit him as hard as you possibly can. Knock him out clean, and let's have some peace … when we get back to peace you will get your money back – with interest.*

Less subtly and rather condescendingly the papers also ran the supposed, pitmatic dialect, comments of a local collier standing on his favourite street corner saying, 'We shud lend wor money to beat the Hun.'

One unlooked-for effect of the impending campaign was that in the weeks before the launch donations to War Savings campaigns were down as people saved themselves for the War Weapons Week. Even so, during the week ending 12 April Ashington had raised £1,875 and Newbiggin £716 (a total of almost £118,000 today).

At the same time as Ashington and district was preparing for the above War Weapons Week, a case before Morpeth magistrates involving a young Ashington woman showed a sadder side of wartime life. Seventeen-year-old Florence Fotheringham had been arrested by police in Morpeth after being found wandering in the town after midnight. At the police station she stated that she had run away from home, not for the first time, and refused to go back. The young woman's parents had been spoken to but had said that they wanted nothing more to do with her, while Florence at first refused to answer the questions of the magistrates. Asked if she had nothing to say she replied, 'No, and I don't care what happens.' Left with little other choice the magistrates stated to Florence that they were faced with having to punish Florence in an effort to make her care about her own future and sentenced her to three months' imprisonment to which the teenager replied, 'I don't care.'[61]

The constant fundraising campaigns did, however, sometimes have the effect of raising war-weariness and of increasing cynicism. The *Morpeth Herald* ran a regular column entitled 'From an Ashington Widow' which purportedly reported on local events and attitudes. Often this was with a comedic intent but equally there was often some cynicism in the article which revealed wider attitudes. In August the column included a short piece talking about charities. It stated that the constant demands for money from flag days and charitable campaigns combined with rising prices meant that the ordinary person was taxed to the extreme. Furthermore, the government campaign to get people to save for the war effort was yet another demand. The writer commented that saving was a simple matter as it just meant making money 'faster than the Government can spend it'.[62]

May opened with yet more bombing, with properties at Glororum Farm (Stannington) and West Clifton Colliery being damaged on the night of 3/4 May, while incendiaries damaged a large portion of Lynemouth and seriously injured two people.[63] Just two nights later there was yet another raid. Bombs were widely scattered over south-east Northumberland and there was serious damage in places. At Bedlington Station a bomb scored a direct hit on 11 Ravensworth Street demolishing two properties while an oil bomb hit and burned down 104 North Row and another set an old colliery on fire. Several other streets were also hit and there was widespread property damage to houses and shops and the electricity was cut off for some time. Thankfully there were no fatalities, although two people were seriously injured and ten suffered minor injuries. Bombs also fell on railway lines around the area and there were others at Seaton Sluice, East Sleekburn, Woodhorn Grange, Longhorsley, Ashington, Blyth, Stamfordham, Mitford and Morpeth. At this last location there was a minor sensation when a

German bomber crashed and burst into flames at St George's Hospital. The five crewmen were detained by the hospital attendants despite at least one of the airmen being armed. RAF Ouston (Stamfordham) also came under attack with 10–12 bombs being dropped before an enemy bomber came down low and made a strafing attack, injuring more than a dozen personnel. By 12.40 am the local police were reporting that the airfield was on fire and that AFS units from around the area were on their way there. As RAF Ouston was the Fighter Sector Headquarters for 13 Group (defending the North and Scotland) this was a serious incident. The airfield, which had only been open for just over two months, suffered damage to hangars and other buildings and at least one aircraft was destroyed.[64] The situation was not helped by the fact that some of the aircraft based at Ouston were attempting to land at the time the raid began.

This was a poor welcome for the Poles of 317 (Wilno) Squadron who had been moved to the airfield on 29 April. It was also a further source of frustration for the Poles who, since formation in February 1941, had grown increasingly irritated at the lack of enemy aerial action over the north-east. Other units using Ouston at the time included 3 Radio Maintenance Unit Calibration Flight and the Hurricanes of 55 OTU which was based at nearby RAF Usworth. On the evening of 2 June, two of 317 Squadron's pilots found and successfully attached a JU88 bomber off the coast, shooting it down just off Tynemouth.

The military came in for criticism shortly after the raid on Ouston when a magistrate declared the military the worst offenders in the case of blackout regulations. Although this was not directly related to the attack of 6/7 May it was made clear that all branches of the military were guilty of failings. In one case, complaints had been made to the local commander and the brigade commander of an offending army unit without any effect and the police were taking the matter to the divisional commander in the hope of some action. The magistrate concurred, declaring that it had been proven that bombs had been dropped in areas where there had been unscreened lights adding that 'In the case of unscreened lights the worse [sic] offenders are the military.'[65]

One of the main organisers behind the many flag days in Morpeth was the Mayoress, Mrs R. Elliott. Having organised many such successful days Mrs Elliott had another triumph when she organised another during the first day of August. Once more the cause was Morpeth Cottage Hospital. On the Saturday morning the mayoress and a group of cheerful helpers paraded around Bridge Street with collecting boxes. With fine weather the people of Morpeth rallied around and the response was described as wonderful, with the first box being quickly filled with the sum of £6. The sum total of £48 18s 6d was counted at the town hall by the mayoress assisted by Mrs W.S. Sanderson, Mrs Bibby and Mrs Mary Dickie.

Wartime marriages were commonplace with young couples anxious to secure happiness despite the dangers of wartime Britain. A particularly patriotic wedding took place at Seaton Hirst Church during the first weekend of August. The couple, Miss Elizabeth Allen and Mr Robert McLean, were both in uniform with Miss Allen having been a WAAF for the previous nine months and the bridegroom and his best man wearing the uniform of the Home Guard. Also wearing the Home Guard khaki was the father of the bride who had served in the Grenadier Guards during the First World War.

We have previously seen the concerns over the activities of young people who were often left to their own devices during the war. In September there were several cases of youngsters from a number of south-east Northumberland communities damaging crops. These included the case of two Bedlington boys, aged 13 and 14, who were found guilty of damaging twenty pikes of hay at Hirst Head Farm. Fining the boys 10s apiece with damages of 5s apiece the magistrate admonished them, saying,

> there is a shortage of agricultural workers ... They are working night and day to get food commodities put into the stores for the winter and you fellows come and pull them down ... You should have been doing more useful work ... This damage going on is a very serious business.[66]

Spurred on by shortages of food and by mischief there were also several cases of turnips being damaged or stolen and the instances of this crime were evidently increasing in frequency. Three Bedlington girls, aged 14 and 13, were found guilty of damaging turnips at Lane End Farm and fined 6s each. The girls were particularly unfortunate as the farm belonged to the District Officer for the War Agricultural Committee, Mr Charles R. Elliott, and he urged for a heavy punishment as a deterrent saying that, given his position, he was keenly aware of the necessity of producing as much food as possible and that warning signs had been placed at farms under the Defence of the Realm regulations. The bench concurred but added that they were 'sorry to see fine girls like you' before them.[67] At the same hearing two Cambois boys aged 12 and 15 were fined 11s each for a similar incident at Town Farm, East Sleekburn, and three Netherton Colliery girls aged 9, 12 and 13 were fined 5s 8d apiece for damaging turnips at South Farm, Nedderton.

Similar cases were also heard involving damage to crops of peas and oats at Brock Lane Farm, East Sleekburn. The farmer, Thomas Patterson, had caught the boys with the peas on them and found that a fair amount of damage had been done to the field. Admonishing the boys, he had told them to keep out of his fields in future. The chairman advised the boys to plant some peas in their own gardens to which one cheekily replied that there were already some peas in his garden and the chairman, who appears to have been slightly amused by this cheek, replied saying that the peas from the field 'must have been a bit sweeter than yours.'[68] It was not only farmers who were vulnerable and the bench also heard the case of two 11-year-old girls from East Sleekburn and Stakeford who were accused of having broken down railings at an allotment and damaged parsnips, peas and turnips: they were fined 5s each and ordered to pay 5s damages. At Choppington it was the apple trees belonging to Choppington Colliery Ltd that became victims when six boys aged between 9 and 14 were convicted of having stolen apples and damaged trees after scaling a 7-10ft fence; each boy was fined the sum of 5s 10d.

Although these cases could be described simply as typical incidents of youth crime and what would now be termed anti-social behaviour, placed into the context of wartime Britain in 1941 they are far more serious and it is no wonder that the magistrates were increasingly concerned over the surge in incidents. The damage to crops was in itself relatively small but it was the fact that each could be seen as weakening the overall national war effort that made stamping it out imperative.

The thefts, however, continued and became of such concern amongst allotment holders in Ashington that members organised themselves to mount night-time guards over their produce. They were reportedly incensed over the repeated thefts which stole valuable produce and which resulted in a great deal of incidental damage. The locals firmly stated that growing such food was as important to the war effort as firing guns and stated to the press that they were appalled that there were some 'of such base morality that they will stoop to pilfering from the gardens of working men'. Recognising that this was different from a few children stealing an armful of turnips they urged local magistrates to impose 'really severe penalties upon any adult person who comes before them on a charge of this kind'.[69]

The urgency of increasing home-grown food supplies was such that, as we have seen previously, local councils were urged to plough up or make available any land that was currently not being used. Shortages of available labour, however, meant that the process was often prone to frustrating delays. The surveyor for Bedlington Urban Council was forced to report in September that the local farmer had failed repeatedly to plough up the land at the proposed Eastgate allotments because of a shortage of labour. Approaches to several other contractors had been made but all had said they had neither the time nor labour to carry out the task and the people who were to work the allotments were growing increasingly frustrated. Highlighting the labour problem the surveyor stated that a similar problem had also arisen at a site in Cambois but the chair immediately ordered the surveyor to make every effort to get the land ploughed, since this had been expected to have been completed 'long before now'.

With the relentless campaigns to grow your own food to support the war effort and the effect that shortages were having it is no surprise that in a large agricultural area like south-east Northumberland the local press ran a regular farming column which, during the war, also gave advice to the more amateur cultivator. Written by a correspondent known as 'Agricola' the weekly column provided all sorts of useful advice and commentary on agricultural and horticultural matters. In September Agricola was praising the efficacies of growing potatoes over wheat. The column alerted farmers to the fact that since most of the country could grow potatoes, whereas wheat was rather more specialised, and that potatoes were less labour intensive and harvesting could be done by unskilled hands (including women and children) one acre of potatoes could be twice as productive as wheat.

The same column gave advice on the benefits and pitfalls of harrowing in spring with Agricola advising that it could do more harm than good on anything but light soil. An extensive 'black list' of species which could damage crops through feeding or inadvertently through their choice of prey was also given, which included the obvious vermin such as rats, rabbits, wood pigeon and grey squirrels but also included rooks, weasels and stoats, jackdaws, little owls, magpies, sparrowhawks, black backed gulls and crows. Agricola said that since many gamekeepers had joined the services it was necessary for those left behind to take on the burden of controlling these species.

While local magistrates (and miners) concerned themselves with the theft of turnips and apples, the members of the local Home Guard units continued with their night vigils against enemy invasion. After its stumbling 1940 start the force was now becoming a viable defensive army with equipment and tactics continually developing. In south-east Northumberland a large number of Home Guard platoons were formed from the workforce of the numerous collieries which dotted the area. Competition between the different collieries had, in the pre-war era, manifested itself on the sports field or in band competitions but service in the Home Guard gave it another outlet. In August one of numerous exercises was held which saw the men of one colliery tasked with launching a night-time assault on one of their neighbours. A journalist from a local paper was one of the witnesses who accompanied the umpires. He described how the men were briefed and then left to their own devices to formulate tactics before he joined the umpires and set out for the target colliery. On the way he became separated from his escort and was thereafter stopped and interrogated whenever he was discovered by a guardsman. The defenders obviously feared fifth column activity and regarded the journalist with extreme suspicion and, while polite, he got the impression that the defenders were keeping a firm eye on him. Indeed, he stated that 'for all their honeyed words, the men of the defending platoon were thinking to themselves: "For two pins, I'd put that blighter in the guard-room."'

The caution of the defenders was understandable as they had already captured three fifth columnists. Two were electricians who had been ordered to infiltrate the colliery and shut down the lights to cause confusion amongst the defenders. Unfortunately for the two men once they reached the time room they were interrogated by members of the defending platoon who knew the goings-on at their own colliery well enough to find flaws in the infiltrators' cover story: these fifth columnists quickly found themselves under arrest. The third was a pit official who had entered claiming that he had been assigned a special job in a specific area of the pit but, once again, the attack failed when he presented his story to a sergeant who was also a pit official who knew there was no such 'special job'. The unlucky official quickly found himself in the company of his fellows.

The attack began with a diversionary assault which was easily repulsed (with prisoners being taken) before the main assault was launched. However, the layout of the colliery, with high slag heaps and buildings offering good vantage points and a tactical advantage, allowed the defenders to maintain the upper hand. One small group of attackers attempted to masquerade as prisoners and got through the initial defences, only for a hand-to-hand melee to erupt with the reporter witnessing rugby tackles, fighting and a couple of minor injuries. As he told his readers 'Home Guard night operations seem to be first-rate opportunities for paying off old scores, and inter-pit rivalry will always ensure enthusiastic give-and-take when the contestants come to grips.'

By the early hours of Sunday morning, the attack had been repulsed and the umpires declared the exercise over. The two groups assembled for a debriefing led by Colonel B. Cruddas, DSO, Major Thomas Norman Sample and the other umpires. Afterwards the attackers set off for home singing and whistling marching tunes despite the early hour and the fact that many of these men had worked on the previous day (some a double shift) and some had to return to work in a few hours' time. The reporter praised the men for their commitment and dedication to this unpaid duty before reassuring readers that, although untested by enemy action, the Home Guard was proving itself more than capable of offering 'stubborn and desperate resistance' to any enemy invasion.[70]

With coal mining so vital to the war effort it is perhaps surprising that it took until August 1941 for the Parliamentary Secretary of the Ministry of Labour to visit such an important hub as Ashington. However, the visit seems to have fallen rather flat with speakers being told that they had to vacate the hall by midday. The *Morpeth Herald*'s Ashington Widow reported that the first parts of the speech by the secretary were ignored by the majority in the hall and by local socialist and trade union leaders. Furthermore, it was said that although the reason for the early end to the meeting was to allow working men to return home for lunch, the real reason 'would probably associate this "old Ashington custom" with the fact that the doors of the pubs open at midday'.

The parliamentary secretary also managed to make an enemy of the local press who had sat dutifully through two long speeches before leaving during the questions and answers session. Once they left, the parliamentarian was ill-advised enough to comment upon them saying that 'now, "the Fascists have gone," he would tell a story'. He then added, somewhat snidely, that he noticed that the reporters had only taken notes on the 'spicy bits'. Somewhat stung by this, the local press retorted saying that they respectfully suggested to 'this lad from Lancashire' that if they had only noted down the 'spicy bits', as he said, then they would have barely written anything at all.[71]

As the war ground on with little good news, morale became a prime concern and there was a further blow as local sporting teams were forced to call it a day due to wartime restraints such as the impacts of recruiting, the blackout, crowd restrictions and funding issues. In August, the footballers of Ashington Football Club were forced to close down for the duration of the war. The Colliers were a proud feature of the town with many locals following them devotedly and, as has been seen previously, the local clubs, including Ashington, were successful in producing players who went on to enjoy professional careers. For Ashington FC the fact that so many of their best and most promising players had joined up, combined with petrol rationing, had created insurmountable difficulties for the club. The local press admitted that sport was of minor importance in wartime but still thought it a pity as football was so important to the British working man; both as a way to maintain morale and as a social safety valve 'for the football season is that period during which the man who has had little differences with his wife over money matters, at the weekend can go and take it out yelling at the referee'.[72]

Although enjoying a more elitist reputation, cricket in the area was also thought unlikely to continue beyond the 1941 season. Once again many of the more able players were now in the forces and the same restriction that had affected football had also affected cricket. The Langwell Crescent Club at Ashington had already lost its captain and chief administrator (this was the newly married Mr Joseph H. Davison who had recently been appointed as head teacher of Stamfordham School) and acknowledged that it would probably not continue after the current season. Morpeth Cricket Club was in a slightly better financial position and continued with fixtures throughout 1941. Local rivalries were always to the fore and a victory over Blyth at Stobhill was warmly welcomed. Even here though the foreshadowing of losing increasing numbers of players to the forces loomed large, with several players being listed alongside their military ranks.

Somewhat surprisingly the hobby of cycling was still actively pursued in some parts of south-east Northumberland despite the war. Broomhill Cycling Club held a large and successful day on Sunday, 3 August when the members of its social section and hard riders' section departed from Broomhill just after 10.00 am. Following a route through Widdrington, Ulgham and Longhirst they reached Morpeth where they paused for their customary rest before setting off up Newgate Street and continuing to Belsay via Mitford, Coldside and Meldon. At Belsay the members of the social section decided to stop for lunch while the others pushed on through Stamfordham and Whittle Dene before pausing at Corbridge for lunch and a rest until 3.00 pm. The hard riders returned on a route which took in Harlow Hill, Dissington and Ponteland before rejoining their comrades at Kirkley where the group had tea. The day was completed with a return journey which took in Saltwick and Tranwell before returning to Morpeth. This long ride will, no doubt, have been undertaken as training for the following week's time trial.

With sports clubs closing down, the men and women of the local Home Guard and ARP units began to organise their own sporting activities. The Home Guard were particularly keen and regular athletics and football events were held. As early as August the Bedlington Home Guard held a sports day which featured several events including 100 yard sprints (for the under 20s), 80 yard sprint (for the over-35s), 440 yard races, sack races, cycle races, tug-o-war, a veterans' race and, interestingly given that there were no female members allowed in the Home Guard, a ladies' race.

As we have seen previously the shortages in wartime Britain led to an active black market in which both civilians and service personnel played a large part. Items such as cigarettes, food and petrol were of particular value and in many cases service personnel were best placed to lay their hands on such commodities. In October, magistrates at Bedlington heard how a locally 'well-respected businessman', James William Keenan (who was a general dealer of 2 Burdon Terrace), was part of a ring which stole 28 gallons of petrol valued at £4 6s (just over £200) from an army petrol store. It was alleged that after meeting Sergeant James B. West and Driver John Ritchie of the Royal Army Service Corps in a local chip shop Mr Keenan had convinced the soldiers to steal the petrol for him. Ritchie testified that West took fourteen tins from the store and handed them to him and he passed them over a wall to Keenan. The police, however, heard of the incident and visited Mr Keenan and upon inspection of his car found the cans of petrol in the boot. Mr Keenan, confronted with the evidence, immediately confessed saying that he had got the petrol and would 'have to take the consequences'.[73]

In mitigation Mr Keenan's solicitor said that he had served in the First World War, earning the Military Medal, and had gone to the store on the 'spur of the moment' at the soldiers' invitation. He argued that as his client was of previous exemplary character he should not be imprisoned for this first offence. Sergeant West pleaded not guilty, claiming that he was drunk on the day in question and could remember nothing of the alleged offence, while Driver Ritchie refused to plead or give evidence. Both soldiers received good character references from their commanding officer. The magistrates handed the soldiers over to the military authorities but, although swayed by the mitigation offered for Mr Keenan, were still eager to make an example of this case and fined him the sum of £30 (£1,360 today).

Although the papers carried news of wartime deaths due to enemy action, there were still everyday civilian tragedies which made the newspapers. In September, there was a perplexing suspected suicide case heard at Ashington Police Station. The deceased was a former Ashington Colliery labourer aged 54 who had been found lying dead on a path between his rented home at the Bungalows, Ellington Road, and Ashington. The deceased's landlady testified that her boarder, Mr Teague, had lived with her for fourteen or fifteen years and had never expressed any symptoms of depression or shown the slightest indication that he intended to take his own life, even on the morning on which he died. Witnesses described finding Mr Teague lying on his back between two gorse bushes with an open and partially empty bottle of Lysol by his side. The doctor who examined him and carried out a post-mortem said that Mr Teague had consumed no alcohol on the day of his death and did not have any major underlying condition. As no suicide note had been left the somewhat perplexed coroner had no alternative but to conclude that Mr Teague had taken his own life by drinking the Lysol while the balance of his mind was temporarily upset.

Although shortages were often at the forefront of the minds of civilians in south-east Northumberland many were also anxious over how loved ones who were in the services were faring, even if they were not in everyday action against the enemy. Eager to reassure these people, to boost morale and to highlight the contribution of volunteers the local press ran a series of articles featuring a recruit to the ATS, Private Gertrude. These articles were always bright and breezy giving reassurances while also seeking to raise morale amongst the civilian population but their primary purpose was in encouraging young women to join the ATS.

In October, Private Gertrude wrote of her recent visit to a centralised army cookhouse in Northumberland. Accompanied by the messing officer, Private Gertrude was intrigued by the smell of freshly baked bread and suggested they investigate. Upon seeing newly baked bread buns she asked in astonishment whether she could expect food like this in the army and was jokingly told 'You bet, you'll be nice and plump by Christmas. We always fatten you poor little recruits up.' Upon asking about another set of buns she was told that they had currants in because it was Chelsea bun day and that the forces got fancy buns every day because 'We have to keep the forces happy.'

Cannily (and keeping an eye on possible recruitment possibilities), Private Gertrude added that she thought she would like to work in such an establishment because she felt it was 'doing something really important helping to feed the troops'. The messing officer, once again clearly intending to boost recruitment, added that although the unit catered for over 1,000 soldiers they had excellent equipment with electric potato peelers and dishwashers along with the presence of male soldiers for the heavy jobs. The surreptitious attempts to boost recruitment continued with Private Gertrude being told that if she impressed with her abilities she might be sent on a cookery course to

Aldershot where she would qualify as a First Class Cook, which would mean that after the war she could find really profitable employment at a hotel or hostel. Private Gertrude then asked the cost of all this and was told it was free, before being reassured that the ATS trained women 'for a dozen or more trades and professions'.[74] Private Gertrude concluded that no young woman would do her post-war chances any harm by joining the ATS. Unsubtly placed at the end of the article was a small advert asking Tyneside and Northumbrian women if they were joining up and to bear in mind that the area had been asked to supply 5,000 recruits immediately.

With the Battle of Britain behind them, the aircrew of RAF Fighter Command began to take the war to the enemy, with fighter sweeps and raids over France. At the end of October, Morpeth lost yet another young man when Squadron Leader John Sample, DFC, was killed in a flying accident. Rested, and trained as a controller in March, Sample was then tasked with forming and commanding 137 Squadron which was

to fly the new twin-engine Whirlwind fighter. Sample flew at least one offensive sweep with 137, during which he claimed to have destroyed several train wagons but four days later, on 28 October, he took two of his young pilots up for formation and attack training. During the course of the flight one of them, Sergeant M.J. Peskett, collided with Sample's aircraft, Whirlwind (P7053) and the tail of Sample's aircraft broke off sending it into an uncontrollable spin. The other pilot, Sergeant J.F. Luing, observed Sample bail out at low level but his parachute did not deploy properly and he landed on the roof of a farm building with his aircraft crashing shortly after.[75] At the time of his death Squadron Leader Sample, DFC, was aged 28. His body was brought back home and he was buried at Bothal churchyard on 3 November.

Squadron Leader John Sample, DFC. A Morpeth Battle of Britain Pilot, Killed in Flying Accident. (Unknown)

Another local RAF casualty came with a particularly sad story. In an effort to boost morale, local newspapers often carried news of local men being promoted or being awarded medals and on 21 November the *Morpeth Herald* carried a short piece informing people that Bedlington pilot Flying Officer Ernest William Tate had been awarded the DFC for his work in attacking an enemy escort vessel off the coast of Norway. Sadly, exactly a week later, Flying Officer Tate (of 220 Squadron, Coastal Command) was killed in action when his Hudson V (AM 799, NR-V) suffered an engine failure while attacking a ship off Stavanger. All four crew were killed with none of the bodies being recovered.[76]

While the activities of the RAF always aroused interest amongst Northumbrians many were keenly aware that the British army was not inactive during this period and was in fact engaged on several distant fronts. One such active theatre of war was the Middle East where the desert war against Italy and Germany was ferocious and demanding, with many Northumbrians involved in various capacities. For a long time, the mining town of Cramlington has enjoyed a reputation for producing boys who have gone on to become excellent footballers. Many north-east born sportsmen joined the forces but one of the most unusual stories has to be that of the inseparable footballing Stephens twins, Alfred and John William (Bill). The brothers had been inseparable since childhood and both played for their hometown club but shortly before the war centre forward Bill attracted the attention of First Division Leeds United and was offered the chance to travel to Yorkshire for a trial at the club. However, unable to face separation from his twin brother, Bill agreed with the proviso that the club also offer a trial to Alfred. After Leeds agreed both the men travelled down and impressed enough to be signed by the Yorkshire club.

Both quickly found themselves pushing for a place in the first team with Bill playing up front and Alfred playing at inside left. Although the war broke out before their debuts could be made, both brothers played for the first team during the 1939-1940 season. The brothers quickly became a 'headache to opposing defenders',[77] especially when both played. Their performances were not quite as effective when one or the other was not in the team.

When war was declared the twins quickly volunteered for service in the army, they joined up together, they went for and passed their medicals together but they were then separated when Bill was posted to Scotland with a cavalry regiment and Alfred remained in Yorkshire as part of the Royal Engineers. The separation played heavily on the minds of both men and caused such consternation in their wider family that their parents contacted the War Office asking if it would be possible to reunite the two.

The War Office was sympathetic to the request and Bill was duly transferred to the Royal Engineers and posted back to Yorkshire where he once again linked up with his brother. The twins completed their training together and were posted to the Middle East where they fought against the Nazis and their Italian allies. By early October, news reached the family that the inseparable brothers had both been taken prisoner and were together in a prisoner of war camp.[78]

At the end of October, the members of Morpeth Corporation elected Councillor James Sharp Jobling as the new mayor of the town. A man of great experience Councillor Jobling had served in the 7th Battalion, Northumberland Fusiliers, throughout the First World War. He had seen active service on the Western Front for three years and rose to the rank of Company Sergeant Major. A councillor for eleven years he had played a significant role both in the council and in the wider Morpeth community. In business he had risen through the ranks of the wine and spirit trade to become a director of R. Edgar & Co. and also carried on the mineral water business of George Young at Chantry Wells.

Given the importance of coal mining to the area it is no surprise that stoppages at some local collieries aroused comment. Seeking to address these concerns, the secretary of the Ashington Miners' Federation, Councillor F. Millican, told a meeting of local senior citizens that the stoppages were in the main caused by inefficiencies in government but reassured the public that the miners were 'doing their utmost' to increase production. The biggest problem was that, with increased production, there was a lack of suitable storage facilities for coal; a possibility that Millican argued the government should have foreseen. The miners, he stated, were most affected by these stoppages and were growing frustrated as they were subjected to calls for increased efforts followed by a colliery being made idle with little or no explanation to those working there.

Although the miners had convinced the government to increase their clothing coupons (correctly arguing that they wore clothes out quickly in their work) official parsimony had decreed that this only applied to those working underground. Surface workers were rightly incensed at this as they argued that their manual work on the surface also led to a great deal of wear and tear on their clothing. By late November the government capitulated and the large majority of surface workers (around 95 per cent) were also given an increase in their clothing allowance.

Given the anxieties suffered by those who had loved ones serving abroad, especially in areas where there was active conflict, it is unsurprising that the news of local men at the front was eagerly devoured and passed on in the small communities of south-east Northumberland. The people of Morpeth received a morale-boosting story about one of their own when news came through of the escape from German hands of Morpethian soldier Sergeant Edward Weallens of the Royal Ordnance Corps. Sergeant Weallens was based in the desert and had been captured by Rommel's Afrika Corps in November. The *Daily Mirror* related how the Morpethian had been held by the Germans for three days and had at one point been questioned by no less than Rommel himself. Asked by the German General if he was 'glad to be out of it' the plucky Sergeant had replied that not only was he not glad to be out of it but that he would 'be glad to be back in it'. Escaping not long afterwards the newspaper could assure the people of Morpeth that the gallant Sergeant Weallens was indeed back in the action,[79] though whether or not Sergeant Weallens' relatives were as cheered is debatable,

As the sinking of vessels off the coast continued unabated, the volunteers of the RNLI saw a huge increase in their workloads.[80] Their work of rescuing sailors and airmen at sea was already dangerous but the threat of mines and air attack made it even more so and the local communities often raised funds to thank the men for their efforts. Because of the massively increased workload the job became almost full time, which created other problems. One of these was the lack of facilities for the men, but once again generosity and the volunteer ethic provided the majority of solutions. In Blyth, for example, funds raised by the Inner Wheel Clubs of Great Britain and Ireland and the WVS led to the purchase of a portable canteen for the use of the Blyth lifeboatmen. The canteen was stocked and run by female volunteers of the WVS. At the ceremony to hand over the canteen, members of the WVS including Countess Grey of Howick (county organiser of the WVS) gave speeches and the mayor, Alderman W.W. Mather, said that the local authority could help with funding. After being congratulated on the work of his men the coxswain of the Blyth lifeboat, J. Wheatley, thanked those who had helped to secure the canteen.

One unlooked-for effect of the war was a growing interest in politics amongst many civilians and forces personnel. As a result of this the treatment and living conditions of many of the subjects of Britain became an area of keen interest. Towards the end of November, the members of Ashington YMCA held a meeting to discuss conditions in India and had Mr V.K. Krishna Menon as guest speaker. Mr Krishna Menon was the editor of a newspaper and a known campaigner for Indian liberty. The speaker described the terrible conditions under which most Indians lived, with high rates of poverty, hunger and illiteracy causing Indian workers to mount frequent strikes demanding better wages and conditions. Mr Krishna Menon explained how, despite government claims that strikers were impeding the war effort, hunger was the root of the problem and that was what was leading to workers going on strike. Throughout his speech Mr Krishna Menon drew links between the conflict with fascism, the cause of liberty and the need for improved rights and living standards in India.

As a result of the meeting, the members of the YMCA along with representatives from the local branch of the Workers' Educational Association (WEA) decided to form a local branch of the Indian League to campaign for an improvement in the standards of living in India.

The Nazi invasion of Russia had seen an outpouring of support for Britain's new ally even though, by the winter of 1941, it looked as though Russia would fall under the Nazi onslaught. Many of the charitable schemes now also focused on raising funds to help this newest ally. Shortly before

Christmas the Red Cross at Bedlington opened a bring-and-buy shop on Front Street. With the shortage of children's toys the many which were displayed prominently in the windows attracted great interest and business was brisk. The organisers made it known that until the end of the year all the proceeds from sales would be given to Mr Churchill's Appeal Fund for Russia. At the opening ceremony the chair of the committee, Father Brietczke, thanked the shop owner for loaning them the premises and said that after the New Year the proceeds would go to the Bedlington Red Cross Committee.

With a third wartime Christmas approaching, many of those who had loved ones in prisoner of war camps were encouraged by the efforts of the Red Cross to provide parcels for these unfortunates. In Morpeth the Red Cross Information Office at 39 Newgate Street put on a display of the contents of their parcels. The charity was making a special effort for Christmas and, while their weekly parcels were also very generous, the contents of the special Christmas parcels reassured both prisoners and relatives that they were not forgotten. Alongside the display was the information that the sending of parcels cost £5,000 (almost £230,000 today) a day and that the total cost so far was £2,500,000 (almost £114,000,000). The popularity of the Red Cross was exemplified by the success of its 'Penny a Week Fund' which during November collected the sum of £42 in Morpeth.

The Northumberland and Durham War Needs Fund continued to attract donations and knitted contributions with the Morpeth Mothers' Union donating sixty-four pairs of socks, twenty-three seamen's jerseys, twenty-one knitted helmets, thirteen pullovers and seven pairs of gloves or mittens in just three months leading up to Christmas. The chairman, Mr G.F. Howell of Morpeth Grammar School, and honorary secretary, Mr D.F. Rae of 13 Newgate Street, were keen to thank the organisations and members of the public who had made contributions. The *Morpeth Herald* listed the following contributions at the end of December:

Ladies' Bowling Club	10s 6d
Ladies' Knitting Party	£2 5s
Bridge Drive	£1 7s 9d
Hospital Supply Depot	9s 6d
Inland Revenue Staff	6s
Rotary Club of Morpeth	10s
Mrs G.A. Catcheside	£7
Employees of Swinney Bros.	£9
Employees of R.L. Jackson & Son	5s
Employees of Supply Stores	4s 6d
Employees of Proctor & Son	1d 8d
Employees of Olivers' Café	3s
Employees of Woolworths	10s

Employees of Pallister's	5s 4d
Employees of J. Smail & Sons	7s 2d
Employees of Bertha Burn	6s 6d
Employees of G. Young & Son	4s
Employees of G. Rutherford & Co. Ltd	11s 8d
Employees of R. Matheson & Son	10s 7d
Employees of Boots, Chemists	6s 2d
Total	£34 14s 4d

The scale of fundraising in south-east Northumberland was phenomenal with it being estimated that, by mid-December, the average Morpethian had saved over £58 (almost £3,000) through subscriptions to National Savings Certificates, Defence Bonds and deposits in Post Office and savings banks.

Food shortages resulted in many struggling to put together a suitably festive meal to celebrate Christmas. Due to the many adverts for wartime recipes and the prevalent spirit of making do, many a Christmas cake in 1941 contained grated carrot and beetroot in place of the very scarce dried fruit. Food in the workplace was also a concern with the Ashington Food Control Committee making disparaging comments about the local miners getting their extra meat ration in the form of pies from the pit canteens. The members of the committee argued that miners in other parts of the country had a far more varied diet yet Ashington miners were buying 48,000 pies every week. Shortly before Christmas the diet did become more varied, with canned meats being made available for purchase and a plan to provide soup made with meat extracts. The soup was to be transported in 10-gallon milk churns which were placed in straw-filled containers and sold at 2d for a half pint along with a piece of bread.

At the time, the Ashington Food Control Committee was also wrestling with the problem of bad eggs being sold by many retailers. People who purchased these eggs and found that the retailer would not replace them with edible eggs were directed to take the eggs to the office of the Food Enforcement Officer at the council chambers. In wry fashion the local press reported that this was good advice but cautioned people that this was not 'an invitation to throw the eggs at the comedians in the council chamber'.[81]

With shortages becoming a major problem and the rationing system becoming more complex the government made some changes to how food supplies were controlled at a local level. A meeting of the Morpeth Rural District Council heard how this would result in the amalgamation of the Morpeth Rural District food office with its Morpeth Borough counterpart. The changes would be effective from 1 January 1942 and new offices were set up at Howard Castle, Dacre Street, Morpeth, with a Mr Primrose being appointed food executive officer.

During the festive season the variety halls, theatres and cinemas were popular sources of entertainment. Customers at the Hippodrome Theatre at

Seaton Hirst were treated to a mixed programme including Harry Hogarth and the Princess Ballroom Orchestra. At the Coliseum picture house in Morpeth the main feature was *Footsteps in the Dark* (1941) starring Errol Flynn while boxing film *The Leather Pushers* (1940) starring Andy Devine and Astrid Allwyn was also showing. The other Morpeth picture house, the Playhouse, was showing another in the Dr Kildare series entitled *My Life is Yours* (better known as *The People vs Doctor Kildare*) starring Lew Ayres and Lionel Barrymore. During Christmas week the Playhouse offered the sentimental and patriotic Battle of Britain film *Dangerous Moonlight* (released as *Suicide Squadron* in the USA) starring Anton Walbrook and Sally Gray. A madcap comedy was also on offer in *The Navy Steps Out* (1941) (originally released as *A Girl, A Guy, and a Gob*) starring George Murphy and Lucille Ball. On Christmas Day both picture houses were showing *Jeannie* (1941) starring Barbara Mullen.

For some families in south-east Northumberland, Christmas saw them receive terrible news of loved ones serving in the Far East. The battle for Hong Kong was brief but extremely fierce with almost 4,500 British and allied troops killed or wounded and 10,000 taken prisoner by the Japanese. The campaign, which began on 8 December (just eight hours after the attack on Pearl Harbor), saw a large number of service personnel and civilians murdered by the Japanese forces. By 13 December the British had been forced off the mainland onto the island and just two days later the Japanese began bombarding their positions. The British were woefully unprepared with no air support (there were only five obsolete aircraft based there) and the majority of the naval support was ordered to fall back to Singapore, leaving the ground forces marooned without adequate support. On 18 December the Japanese landed in the harbour with few losses and two days later the British forces were split and running out of water. By the afternoon of Christmas Day it had become obvious to all that the British and their allies could not hope to hold out and they agreed to surrender the island.[82]

It seems likely that at least two men from south-east Northumberland may have been amongst these unfortunates as 25-year-old Gunner Henry Brown, 12th Coast Regiment, Royal Artillery, was killed on or around Christmas Eve and has no known grave, instead being commemorated on the Sai Wan Memorial. Private Joseph Thomas Smith, a 26-year-old of the 2nd Royal Scots, was killed on 15 December and is also commemorated on the Sai Wan Memorial. Another 26-year-old, Private William Mitchell Logan, 1st Middlesex Regiment, was also killed on Christmas Eve and is, again, commemorated on the same memorial. It is known that several men from these units were amongst the victims of the various massacres and with many of the bodies being cremated or otherwise disposed of by the Japanese it has proven impossible to accurately account for many of the victims.[83]

There were two more tragic losses on 23 December when the Defensively Equipped Merchant Ship (DEMS) SS *Shuntien* was sunk by *U-559* while en route from Tobruk to Alexandria. The vessel was transporting between 800 and 1,000 German and Italian prisoners of war escorted by 40 men of the 1st Durham Light Infantry (DLI) when, at approximately 7.00 pm, she had her stern blown off by a torpedo. The ship sank within five minutes with no chance to launch her lifeboats. Amongst those guarding the prisoners were 28-year-old Private Alan Richardson of Kenton North and 25-year-old Private Albert Gregg of Netherton Colliery. Both lost their lives and are commemorated, because their deaths occurred at sea in waters not associated with the major campaigns, on the Brookwood 1939-1945 Memorial in Surrey.[84]

1942: The End of the Beginning

Although the most important industries in south-east Northumberland were coal mining and agriculture, the coastal towns and villages relied largely on fishing. Many of the trawlermen of the area were members of the Royal Naval Reserve and were serving (the majority aboard minesweeping trawlers) in the RN. Others who had been left behind found a captive market for the fish they landed and large profits could be made but the work, very dangerous in peacetime, was even more perilous during the war as mines and enemy aerial attacks took a deadly toll of the north-east fishing fleet. At Newbiggin-by-the-Sea the fishing community fished largely from cobles and the work involved the entire community. The women of Newbiggin worked incredibly hard launching and retrieving the cobles, carrying loads of fish and also hauled the lifeboat when it was needed.

Newbiggin women retrieve cobles on a wheeled undercarriage. (The Sphere)

Newbiggin women haul the lifeboat to its shed. (The Sphere)

Minesweeping trawlers off the North-East coast. (The Sphere)

Given the importance of the south-east Northumberland coalfield to both the local area and the national war effort it was no surprise that a perceived shortage of miners coming through was worrying the authorities. Even though many young boys preferred the perceived glamour of the armed forces there were those who saw themselves pursuing a career in the mines. At Ashington a scheme had been set up in 1941 to train such boys. The boys were given extensive instruction in pit machinery, underground working methods, safety lamps, ventilation, first aid, mining history and even good citizenship. Practical instruction was given in a special training gallery and the scheme proved a great success.

The initial enthusiasm and chaos surrounding the formation of the LDV/Home Guard led to many nebulous legal areas concerning duties and the possession of private firearms. Some police divisions in south-east Northumberland (especially those in mining districts it appears) were

A class of young boy miners in the training gallery at Ashington. (The Sphere)

Young trainee boy miners haul tubs. It was important to know how to use such equipment safely. (The Sphere)

especially frustrated by these perceived breaches of the law and were notoriously zealous in enforcing what they saw as the law. In March, the magistrates at Ashington saw two cases involving members of the Home Guard who had been charged with illegal possession of pistols without the necessary licences. The first was that of George Hindle (45), a horsekeeper from 11 Eleventh Row, Ashington, who was also a non-commissioned officer (NCO) in the Home Guard. Upon questioning by PC Givens, who had established that Mr Hindle was indeed a member of the Home Guard, it was revealed that Mr Hindle had possessed a revolver since 1919 but it had been inoperable until he joined the Home Guard and asked his officer if it would be advisable to get it re-activated. His commanding officer assured him that he would be entitled to do so as the Firearms Act did not apply to the Home Guard according to War Office instructions.

The second case was almost identical and involved Samuel Templeton Young (48) of 26 Pont Street, Ashington, and again the officer involved was PC Givens. Calling at Mr Young's home he had asked his wife if her husband possessed a gun and she told him he had a pistol before showing him the weapon. PC Givens said that he would be charged with possession of the gun.

Once again this was a case of a member of the Home Guard having an old pistol mended and used exclusively for Home Guard duties.

The bench dismissed both cases but charged the accused a small amount in costs and accepted the suggestion of the superintendent in charging these costs after the officer alleged that such cases were problematic and that the two men should have followed the correct procedure by applying to the authorities for registration (even though, legally, they did not have to). It is interesting that both cases involved the same charging officer and one wonders if PC Givens perhaps had an axe to grind with the two men or with the Home Guard in general.

It was certainly true that at times the Home Guard took matters into their own hands and raised the ire of the local population they were there to protect. At the end of September, a lieutenant in the Home Guard at Newbiggin was brought up before the magistrates at Ashington charged with having assaulted a 10-year-old boy, Cyril Charles Firmin, by striking him twice on the buttocks with a stick. The evidence given suggested that the boy had been warned away from a Home Guard beach defence on several occasions and that his father had also told him not to go there but that on the day in question he and another boy had once again climbed upon the structure and a witness testified to them causing damage. The officer, Lieutenant Joseph Murray, admitted to having struck the boy twice to ward him off but denied doing so violently (contrary to the evidence of a woman who was passing at the time) and stated that he believed that it was more useful to do so than prosecuting the parents for damage to the Home Guard equipment. The magistrates admitted that the defendant had no right to strike the boy but in view of the mitigating factors fined him the nominal sum of 10s.

With the football season largely suspended the many military formations in Britain took up some of the slack and fixtures between regular units, Home Guard teams and even representatives from ARP services and works were commonplace. In September, the Pegswood Home Guard scored a victory over their regular colleagues, despite being outnumbered eleven to eight, when they beat a team from the Royal Engineers 4-3.

Fundraising in aid of the war effort continued throughout the year with large and small donations to a massive variety of causes. In early March, Ashington held its 'Warship Week' which aimed to raise the sum of £100,000. The enthusiasm of the town's inhabitants can clearly be seen when donors included a small girl who raised a guinea by raffling off a toy pixie which she had made herself. Other ingenious methods included a local organisation which promised to donate a war savings certificate for each baby born during the week. Unfortunately, only four women came forward: Beryl Morgan (53 Alexandra Road); Elsie Stafford (45 Rowlington Terrace); Leslie McLean (29 Katherine Street); and Patricia Duff (8 Beatrice Street). By the end of the week the aimed-for sum had been exceeded by £20,503 and the town was given the honour of adopting the minesweeper HMS *Blackpool*.[85]

Throughout February, Northern District held a competition to collect salvaged paper to aid the war effort. Held over Northumberland, Durham and Cumberland the competition raised significant funds and prizes were offered for districts which collected the most paper. Morpeth rallied to the event and finished second overall and was subsequently awarded a prize of £250. The council's salvage committee decided to allocate the prize money to eight separate charities, in line with half having to go to national charities and the other half to local concerns. Alderman Sanderson praised the Mayor, Councillor James S. Jobling, for the way in which he had engaged in supporting the salvage effort and for donating the prize money so fairly.

Disbursement of Prize Money from Salvaged Paper Collection

Charity	Donation Amount
Red Cross	£50
Mrs Churchill's Aid to Russia Fund	£25
RAF Benevolent Fund	£25
Soldiers, Sailors and Airmen's Families Association	£25
Morpeth Cottage Hospital	£60
Morpeth Dispensary	£25
Royal Victoria Infirmary (Newcastle)	£25
Local Nursing Fund	£15

The cheque was handed to the mayor on 12 March at a Minstrel Concert held at the town hall in Morpeth to support the Morpeth and District 'Warship Week'. In accepting the cheque Councillor Jobling thanked the people of Morpeth for their amazing spirit in collecting so much salvaged paper. The effort, he said, came from every quarter of the town, from all age groups and from numerous organisations. He especially praised the ARP services, the Boy Scouts and the Girl Guides. The salvage staff, under the leadership of the borough surveyor, Mr F.K. Perkins, had made an especially valued contribution and without their efforts the collection would not have been nearly as successful. The mayor concluded his speech by urging Morpethians to get behind the 'Warship Week' and ensure that the total raised topped the record amount of the previous year.

Even amongst all the fundraising efforts for the continuing war effort there were still successful collections held for providing goods for those Northumbrians who had been unfortunate enough to find themselves prisoners of war. Many of these had been in captivity since 1940, being taken during the blitzkrieg of France. In February, the local newspapers highlighted the experiences of Morpeth doctor Captain Hugh Dickie who had been taken prisoner while serving with the 51st (Highland) Division as medical officer for the 7th Royal Northumberland Fusiliers. Before the war, Dr Dickie had practised as a partner in the practice of Dickie & Davidson and had lived at Greystoke. In the same month a whist drive held at Miss Dixon's Café in Morpeth raised £20 10s for the Local Prisoners of War Fund.

During June a large open meeting was held by the WVS at Morpeth Town Hall. Presided over by Lady Grey, the main speaker was the regional organiser for Northumberland, Durham and the North Riding, Mrs Stewart-Reed. In her speech Mrs Stewart-Reed was at pains to point out the many duties of the WVS and the contribution made to civil defence. Mrs Stewart-Reed was also keen to encourage more women to join the organisation in Morpeth as there was presently only a small group, although it did sterling work. She told listeners how some members had agreed to become part of a housewives' section which would entail them remaining in their houses during air raids, displaying a blue card to let those who need help known that they could go there for food or other aid. The main theme of Mrs Stewart-Reed's lecture, however, was on the need for thrift. She stated firmly that the 'urgent need at the moment was to save everything they could and waste nothing'.[86]

The WVS also raised substantial funds and organised morale-boosting events, manning stalls and organising games for children. In July, the Lynemouth branch hosted just such a garden fete (at the Welfare Ground) at which there were a variety of stalls, refreshments and games. The event was in aid of the Red Cross and the speakers praised the generosity of the people of Lynemouth in contributing to this organisation.

The cinemas of south-east Northumberland remained popular, with increasing numbers of drama/propaganda films being shown regularly. In March, the Coliseum in Morpeth was showing the ever-popular Leslie Howard in the 1941 film *Pimpernel Smith* which was an update of the actor's performance in *The Scarlet Pimpernel* (1934) and which moved the action to pre-war Nazi Germany where Howard's character, archaeologist Professor Horatio Smith, uses his cover of being on a dig to explore the Aryan origins of German civilisation to free political prisoners. The film found a warm welcome from wartime British audiences and was the third most popular film of 1941.

Amongst the rough and tumble tasks that fell to the volunteer land girls was sheep dipping. Many were completely unused to this procedure, which involved harsh chemicals and strong and obstreperous sheep who intensely disliked being manhandled and submerged. Despite the massive contribution made by the women of the Land Army there was still opposition to them in some quarters. Ashington Council, like many local authorities, had seen its manpower denuded by enlistments and call-ups to the armed forces and it was suggested that the employment of a Land Girl at Hirst Park might ease the situation. However, it was reported that 'the introduction of a land girl, in breeches and leggings, into the gardening staff at Hirst Park would be viewed with some alarm in certain quarters.' Writing tongue in cheek the 'Ashington Widow' said that the fear was probably that a feminine influence would be disturbing to the staff and park-goers but suggested that applications could be accompanied by a photograph so that 'anything remotely approaching a glamour girl could be rigorously excluded'.[87]

In June, a Women's Land Army rally was held at Morpeth Town Hall for members from the East Bellingham, Castle Ward, Newcastle and Morpeth districts. After visiting a local cinema, the girls were entertained by the county committee. A speech by Colonel Cruddas praised their efforts and highlighted the importance of agriculture to the war effort; reassuring the girls that 'people were beginning to realise that agriculture was a very skilled trade' and that they were playing a very big role in this vital effort. After his speech, Colonel Cruddas handed out awards for achievement and long service. Demonstrating the rigours of being a land girl, the vote of thanks was proposed by a woman who was a member of the Timber Corps (otherwise known as Lumber Jills or Pole Cats).

It was not only the Women's Land Army who were helping out in agriculture, however. Across Northumberland, schoolchildren and women were volunteering to help farmers to gather in their harvest as, despite high wages for agricultural labourers, labour was short and the past three years had seen an additional 6 million acres of old grassland ploughed up and added to the nation's tillage total. This zealous approach was no doubt aided by the government's promise to pay £2 per acre for every additional acre that was ploughed up, sown and put into production.[88]

The vital importance of the farming industry of rural Northumberland was highlighted by repeated praise of the farmers who in many cases had ploughed up previous pasture and meadowland in order to grow a greater tonnage of arable and vegetable crops. In September, the people of the area were encouraged to be told that the potato and root vegetable crop in the county had been extremely good and promised to 'excel all records'. It was not only farmers who came in for praise, so did the many amateur gardeners who had turned over their allotments, gardens and waste ground to producing food during the crisis. In particular, a group at Morpeth were praised for their efforts in experimenting with the production of two potato crops from one piece of ground by sowing again as soon as the early crop was lifted in June.

The huge increase in the workload for Northumbrian farmers resulted in an expansion of mechanisation in the area. The most visible sign of this was the massive increase in tractor usage.[89] Fordson was a particularly popular brand and with the increased workload that these tractors were having to undergo local garages mounted continuous campaigns urging farmers to ensure that their tractors were kept in working order. Indeed, some mechanics placed adverts telling farmers it was their patriotic duty to ensure that their tractors, and other equipment, was regularly maintained. The Morpeth firm of S. Jennings Ltd placed regular adverts notifying farmers that it was a specialised Fordson tractor repair and maintenance facility and that using its service to ensure that their tractors were in good condition would guarantee a longer service life and allow farmers to save precious fuel.

In addition to the widespread use of machinery farmers were strongly encouraged to make increasing use of nitrogen-based fertilizers and to top dress cereal crops, both by the local War-Ag and by constant adverts from the Ministry of Agriculture. Indeed, certain crops were covered by a governmental general order which meant that farmers were required by law to fertilize with at least 1cwt of nitrogen fertilizer. These adverts also exhorted farmers and farmworkers to put their all into their efforts on the land and to help out their neighbours if they were in need.

Despite a widespread public focus on the 'Ploughing Up' and 'Dig for Victory' campaigns, the production of meat and milk was still of prime importance to the national war effort. The government had agreed before the war that it would be sole purchaser for milk and some other products and would buy them at regulated prices. Although this led to stability for farmers it also led to the inevitable grumbling over the price rates as the war went on. Despite the 1939 promise of Reginald Dorman-Smith, then Minister for Agriculture, that livestock farmers would be provided with sufficient feed, there was growing unrest in south-east Northumberland by 1942. Dairy farmers were particularly discontented and came in for criticism at Morpeth in April when a meeting of local dairy farmers took place at the town hall. The president of the meeting, Mr A.B. Howie of Eshott Brocks, informed his fellows that unless they improved production then the local War-Ag would put compulsory measures in place. Mr Howie appealed to his fellow farmers' patriotism saying that 'in these days of stress and anxiety' they should not quibble at regulated prices and that they 'should cease grousing and get on with the job'.[90]

On a more conciliatory note the technical advisor from the Northumberland War-Ag, Mr H.C. Pawson, stated that as he saw it the biggest problem was the failure to provide a suitable arrangement of cropping on some farms, which resulted in a lack of feed for livestock for milk production. He advised the meeting that the only way forward was for individual farms to become as self-sufficient as possible in order to increase milk production to the demanded levels.

In the same edition of the *Morpeth Herald,* which documented the above meeting, the newspaper's agricultural correspondent, 'Agricola', wrote in a similar vein offering advice to Northumberland farmers. He stated that with the successes of the ploughing up campaign had come a realisation amongst many farmers that grass had an important part to play in crop rotation with leys (arable land used in the previous season) being very productive when turned out to grass and, indeed, an improvement on established pasture. 'Agricola' was at pains to point out that this growing realisation was particularly important to dairy farmers, as good fresh grass was the best food available.

With increasing losses of food in the Atlantic, Dorman-Smith's successor, Robert Hudson, was keenly aware of the dire position in which Britain found itself by 1942 and constantly encouraged those working the land to put every effort they could into increasing production during the year; despite acknowledging the fact that the 'Ploughing Up' campaign had to all extents run its course. 'Agricola' advised that the key to this was an improvement in overall farm management but cautioned strongly against overdoing cultivation in this increasingly mechanised era. He held up the overworking of turnip fields which left the land dry and barren for future seasons but criticised the 'tens of thousands of acres' which were waterlogged because of poor drainage. He advised farmers, landowners and workers that ditches were the solution to the problem and told them to 'fight to the last ditch'.[91]

The extremely severe weather of the winter of 1941-2 had damaged some bean crops and 'Agricola' gave advice on how to salvage these valuable crops along with advising farmers on caring for seedlings, especially in view of the shortages of seed that were impacting the industry. The agricultural correspondent reserved especial praise in his column for the work of the Women's Land Army and all women working the land over the last few months, arguing that their contribution was 'second to none in national importance' and saying 'Driving a tractor, or cleaning out a milking shed at half-past five in the morning was no joyride during recent months, but members of the WLA could, and did, do it.' Commenting on some of the early antipathy towards the land girls, 'Agricola' said that this had largely died down and that 'there is no reason for thinking that a woman need do any less work, or such work less satisfactorily, than a man'. Farmers, he added, were accepting the dilution of agricultural labour as a benefit in trying times rather than as a 'necessary evil'.[92]

Although there was resentment in some farming circles towards the War-Ag most farmers accepted it as a wartime necessity and even welcomed the input from the War-Ag in organising demonstrations of new techniques and technologies. The aforementioned Mr Howie of Eshott Brocks, Felton, played a substantial role in the work of the War-Ag and in encouraging developments in local farming practices. For example, in mid-August he agreed to the use of his land for a demonstration in new practices in arable dairy farming which had been organised by the War-Ag. Adverts placed in the local press invited not only all local farmers but also farmworkers to the demonstration.

Crime continued throughout the year and at Blyth drunkenness amongst women was frequently commented upon in some circles. The meeting of the Bedlington Licensing Sessions in Blyth in February proposed several measures to counter this worrying trend. Firstly, it wanted publicans to be more aware of their responsibilities in preventing drunkenness amongst women, especially young women. Secondly, the sessions demanded the hiring of policewomen to engage with the women of the district to show them the errors of their ways. The chair, Mr J. Goulding, clearly abhorred the fact that there had been a small increase in drunkenness amongst women and stated that it was no secret what was going on in the town and that anyone walking through Blyth would 'see women coming out of public houses in daylight. You will see more young women than men … It is simply dreadful. The magistrates are very much alarmed'. Mr Goulding concluded that in his opinion 'It is pathetic to see a young woman come out of a public house the worse for drink.'[93]

The large numbers of soldiers who were billeted in and around Morpeth could sometimes be a source of trouble, with many finding themselves before the local magistrates for a variety of offences; many involving drink. In February one such soldier, Daniel O'Brien, was sentenced to three months' imprisonment for the theft of a handbag and several other items from Stobhill resident Frances Wilson. Ms Wilson stated to the police that on the night of 30 January she had visited the Black Swan and stayed until closing time at 10.00 pm. Upon leaving she had her handbag stolen from her by O'Brien who ran off. The accused alleged that Ms Wilson, whom he knew only as Flo, had approached him begging for drink and had become abusive when he declined. Ms Wilson vehemently denied this.

Two days later Ms Wilson, accompanied by PC Kelman, attended a military parade of over 100 soldiers and Ms Wilson positively identified O'Brien as the soldier responsible for the theft. Although he initially denied any knowledge he later confessed to the police that he had indeed stolen the bag and after fleeing found himself at a fish shop in Newgate Street where he opened the bag and took 10*s* before disposing of the handbag. O'Brien stated that he had had several drinks and could not remember the exact details of the night. Upon investigation it was discovered that O'Brien was no stranger to the courts. A Glaswegian, he had as a young man entered Glasgow University to train as a teacher but lasted only a few months. He had been married (he was separated at the time of the events in Morpeth) but he and his wife had been convicted of housebreaking in 1935 and he had served time in prison. While he was in prison his wife was found guilty of bigamy after she married an Indian gentleman. Before the war he was employed as a travelling vacuum cleaner salesman but he had joined the army. His career as a soldier must have followed a similar line as his commanding officer told the court that O'Brien 'had a very bad military record, in fact he had no redeeming feature about his character' and that 'The army does not want this man.'[94]

The same sitting heard the case of another Glaswegian soldier, Joseph McQuade, who was fined the sum of £1 for the theft of a chair from a dance hall at Red Row, Broomhill. McQuade had been caught red-handed by a police constable, to whom he had been very abusive, and could offer no defence other than that he was drunk. Like O'Brien he had a long list of criminal convictions having been charged with twelve offences in Glasgow in 1934 before being sent to a borstal three years later for housebreaking. In 1940 he had received a three-month prison sentence for the same crime and a year later a further month, once again for housebreaking. Somewhat surprisingly the officer present at the hearing said that the army would take McQuade back and the bench therefore ordered the fine to be paid immediately.

We have seen previously how dangerous the job of coal mining was during the war and in April the coroner heard a case detailing the death of an 18-year-old lad from Newbiggin. John William Lupton was employed as a surface worker at Newbiggin Colliery when he was struck by some coal tubs and had his leg severed as he attempted to cross the rolleyway. There seems to have been arguments for neglect on the part of the man employed to detach the tubs from the rope and from the colliery management who had failed to repair at least one hole in the rolleyway. The coroner heard how Lupton, described as an energetic and keen young man, had caught his foot in such a hole and the tubs had struck him. However, the coroner reached a verdict of accidental death but told the colliery manager that safety arrangements and procedures must be improved. The victim's father stated that his son wore glasses and that, although he had received safety training and certificates, 'his son was doing a man's job, otherwise the accident might not have happened'.[95] With manpower shortages those working in the mines were increasingly very young men or older men who may even have retired before the war; during the next year youngsters would even be conscripted into the industry.

Safety in the mines of the north was becoming a great concern and there was especial unease over the dramatic decline in interest in safety training amongst the younger workers, with a marked downturn in enrolments. The Divisional Inspector of Mines pointed out that in 1941 there had been ten fatalities amongst boys employed in northern collieries and that of these only one boy had received safety training and he had been killed by events outside his control. Recruitment of boys into the mines was declining partly because of the reluctance of parents to allow their sons to enter into what they knew was such a dangerous occupation. The inspector stated in his report that there had been 149 fatal accidents in northern mines during 1941: 48 of them in Northumberland.

Fatal Accidents in Northern Mines (Northumberland, Durham, Cumberland and North Riding)

Year	Fatalities
1939	124
1940	165
1941	149

Not everyone appreciated the efforts of the miners. Writing in the *Morpeth Herald* the 'Ashington Widow' expressed her disdain for many in the industry after they had received a pay rise in the summer of 1942. Despite the government expressing the hope that the increased wages might see an increased effort and increased production, the writer was extremely dubious, stating that they were 'set for a disappointment'. She complained that many of the men said they were already doing all they could, while others blamed the food they were given or the management (while the management blamed the miners themselves). The writer stated that it was 'an open secret that as many as a quarter of the actual coal producers at some of the local collieries are absentees on Mondays'.[96]

With the massive increase in turnover at local shipyards and repair yards and a lack of manpower to monitor comings and goings it was increasingly possible for men employed in positions of relatively minor power and influence to illegally exploit the wartime situation in order to make huge profits. In many cases this involved the rerouting of materials destined for the war effort in order to sell them on the black market or to reduce private business costs.

A serious case was heard throughout August, which referred to just such a case at Blyth where nine men, all employees of Blyth Shipbuilding & Dry Docks Company Ltd, were tried on seventy-eight separate charges of theft, bribery, conspiracy, fraud and receiving stolen goods. Blyth Shipbuilding & Dry Docks Co. Ltd was a relatively small yard but had a history dating back to 1811. It had closed in 1930 due to the depression but was reactivated in 1937 and from then until 1942 had built a large number of minesweepers and boom defence vessels for the Admiralty. In 1942 the company received orders for several frigates and from then until the end of the war the company constructed five 'River' class frigates and seven 'Castle' class frigates along with three 'B' Type coasters (of 1,200 tons), a large tank landing craft and two tugs.[97] In 1941, the repair yard had also overseen the conversion of a German cargo-liner, the *Hannover*, which had been captured in the West Indies into the Royal Navy's first escort carrier, HMS *Audacity*.

Several of the accused held positions of influence: John Pascoe (45) was an agent (presumably for an assurance or transport company) from North Shields; Percy Lewis Stokoe (70) was the dock manager; Dr John Stokoe (40), the son of Percy, was described as the Medical Officer for Health, Blyth; while Frederick Terence James (47) was foreman painter at the company. The remaining accused were all brothers: Charles Wintersgill (52) was the secretary and general manager at the company; Henry Wintersgill (63), a slate merchant from Stockton; Thomas Wintersgill (50), a builder from Stockton; Benjamin Wintersgill (57), another slate merchant from Stockton; and Joseph Wintersgill (47), a haulage contractor from Northallerton.

The trial, which took place at Newcastle Assizes, began in late July and did not end until a month later. The first cases to be heard were against

Pascoe, James, Percy Stokoe and Charles Wintersgill, who all pleaded not guilty. Early in the trial it was revealed that the company had undertaken a lot of Admiralty work during the war and had been paid the sum of £197,000 (£8,372,500 today). The district accountant for the Admiralty, David Morgan, gave evidence as to this and also alluded to the system of having an Admiralty employed recorder present for much of the time at the company to check on the flow of labour and supplies into the yard and to monitor work on Admiralty contracts but, said Mr Morgan, he would not concern himself with sub-contracts.

The men seemed to have been siphoning off supplies of use primarily to the building trade while Percy Stokoe was also alleged to have received supplies for the house he was building at Todburn. The bench heard that the chief costs and accounts clerk from the yard, Mr Richard W. Durrant, had 'checked accounts and ascertained prices of various articles from other firms [and that he had] ... performed certain small services for Pascoe and it was not unreasonable he should receive payment'.[98] It would appear that Mr Durrant had indeed been rewarded by Pascoe for he admitted under questioning that he had received a portable wireless set, a paraffin lamp, a pair of binoculars and a bottle of whisky but in seeking to deflect any idea that these were in fact payments for services rendered he added that he considered that he still owed Mr Pascoe for the goods.

Evidence was also heard that an attempt had been made to pass false accounts for paint for use on ships. The assistant secretary of the company, Alan Greig, alleged that although paint had not increased significantly in price it seemed that the company accounts were attempting to reason that materials for a ship built in 1938 cost just £295 while the 1941 accounts priced a similar ship at £813; an increase of over 275 per cent (in today's prices this meant a profit of over £22,000 from the 1938 figure). Mr Greig concluded in his evidence that there was nothing 'which could possibly account for the rise'.

Another allegation arose over the alleged removal of brand new timber from the yard for the use of building work on Mr Stokoe's bungalow at Todburn. Mr Durrant, under examination from Stokoe's solicitor, said that when he heard the police make this allegation it appeared to him that Mr Stokoe knew nothing about it. The chairman of the company, Mr Robert Stanley Dalgliesh, gave evidence that he had known Percy Stokoe for some years and had always found him to have a good and honest character and that it was commonplace for useless timber to be lying around the yard, that this timber was valueless, and that Stokoe had the authority to clear out timber of this type from the yard.

Next to give evidence was the largest shareholder in the company, Sir Arthur M. Sutherland, who testified that he had never given anyone authority to release shipbuilding materials to Pascoe and that he had also never authorised the use of the yard lorry or its petrol for the purpose of ferrying building materials to Mr Stokoe's bungalow. Cross-examining, and clearly attempting to muddy the waters, Pascoe's solicitor asked Sir Arthur what he and the other directors had done to justify several payments for special expenses which were in the accounts. Sir Arthur explained that in the years before the war the company had experienced financial difficulties (losing £143,000 or over £6,000,000 today) and that the payments were for travelling and other expenses. The solicitor then asked if Sir Arthur could justify a payment in 1940 of £200 to Mr Dalgliesh and £100 to himself for company work on three ships. Sir Arthur answered that the payment to him was for hosting several luncheons and other miscellaneous expenses. At this point in the exchange the Judge, Mr Justice Cassels, asked what the purpose was in this line of questioning to which the solicitor, Mr Morley, replied that it showed 'that the yard was carelessly managed, that money was being bandied about and accepted by everybody'.[99] The judge was unimpressed and said that the court shouldn't be used in order to 'cross-examine directors'.

Although the judge wasn't impressed, the court heard from Charles Wintersgill (a director as well as secretary and general manager) that he regularly signed weekly wage cheques which were blank and that he had no knowledge of what was being paid to whom. The company's cashier, James Bohill, stated that between September 1939 and April 1942 he was aware of £88,902 11s (over £3,778,000 today) being paid, all but £1,635 of it in cash, to Pascoe and that this money came from the weekly wage cheque that was signed by Wintersgill. Detective Sergeant Taylor stated that the total sum in bank notes recovered from the accused was £306,937 (or approximately £13,044,000 today); the police also argued that Pascoe had paid bribes to James amounting to £2,500.

After a lengthy trial lasting sixteen days all four men were found guilty although the judge deferred sentencing until after the remaining men's cases had been heard. Pascoe was found guilty of three charges of conspiracy, seven of bribery, five of false pretences and one of receiving; he was found not guilty on two charges of bribery and two of receiving. Charles Wintersgill was found guilty of three charges of conspiracy, five of false pretences and one of larceny; he was not guilty of two other charges of larceny. James was found guilty of three counts of conspiracy, two of bribery and four of false pretences. Percy L. Stokoe was found guilty of three charges of conspiracy and three of false pretences; he was found not guilty on two other charges of false pretences and three of larceny.

The trial of the remaining defendants, the four remaining Wintersgill brothers and John Stokoe, began the next day with all of the men facing charges of receiving and Dr Stokoe, Joseph, Benjamin and Henry were also charged with conspiracy. He court heard how the charges all pertained to the removal of materials from the yard and transportation to one or other of the Wintersgills' properties where they were unloaded but not paid for. One of the lorry drivers employed by the yard, Henry Wigham, testified that since 1939 he had made twenty-seven journeys to Stockton (where the remaining Wintersgills lived) and had delivered items including coal, furniture, aluminium, old timber and cement slabs from the yard and dumped them at the back of Benjamin Wintersgill's house. He claimed that 'No one told him where to take the coal' "It was more or less a standing order."'[100] Wigham also testified that on at least one occasion he had taken a cargo of aluminium sheets to the premises of Thomas Wintersgill but also said that the timber he had ferried was old and included items such as hatch covers and that the cement, to him, had looked second-hand.

James Bohill, cashier, was again questioned, this time regarding a walnut burr furniture suite which it was alleged had been made in the shipyard but sent to Benjamin Wintersgill at his Stockton address. Bohill agreed that the firms of B. Wintersgill & Son and T. Wintersgill Ltd had supplied materials and that accounts were kept for suppliers and those receiving goods. He was then asked if there was any mention in the accounts for the two companies for several items as follows: aluminium sheets; concrete slabs; a jib crane; pitch pine planks; hatch covers; coal; and 4x2 timber. Mr Bohill said that there were no accounts for these items. When asked if an account would have been kept if they had been getting supplies from the yard he answered in the affirmative but repeated that there were no such entries in the accounts.

Mr Bohill agreed that the secretary and manager had a suite of furniture made up in the yard's joiners' shop but said that there was nothing wrong with that. Upon being asked once more if he was certain he could see nothing wrong in this the witness provoked laughter in the court when he answered 'Perhaps you didn't want one.' The prosecution then established that the wood had been ordered and paid for by the company and after declaring that the yard built and repaired ships asked Mr Bohill if it was correct that the yard did not make furniture. Mr Bohill answered that the yard did not make furniture for ships but seems to have been implying that some private manufacture of furniture had taken place before. He also said that there would not have been any difficulty in making such a suite of furniture for Charles Wintersgill and the prosecution stated that Mr Wintersgill would surely have been expected to have at least paid for the labour involved in the construction of the furniture to which Mr Bohill answered that 'The labour could have been gotten over' but admitted that he was not aware of any payments or arrangements with those who built the furniture.[101]

By the time the judge summed up Joseph and Henry Wintersgill had been acquitted (Dr Stokoe also seems to have been acquitted later). Mr Justice Cassels' summing up of what was a complex and important case took over three hours on the morning of 26 August. Cassels told the jury that they needed to reach a decision on whether the offences were down to criminality or slackness and incompetence and that since in the case of Stokoe there was no suggestion he had ever got anything out of the alleged thefts they were tasked with determining if he was a thief or if he was only acting upon orders from superiors.

The jury returned quite quickly and all the remaining men were found guilty with Mr Justice Cassels handing down sentences the next day. Determining that Pascoe had been the ringleader of the corruption, the judge in handing down a sentence of seven years' imprisonment and fines totalling £4,600 said that Pascoe had 'set out to corrupt that shipyard and its employees, and thereby were able to obtain large sums of money for goods that you did not supply'. He also declared that Pascoe had 'built a payroll of men from the manager downwards … [and that] from being a small man commercially, you leapt into a strong financial position' and that he had placed the money into his 12-year-old daughter's accounts in order to 'enjoy the proceeds of your crime'.[102] It was revealed after the sentencing that Pascoe had served a number of terms of imprisonment for a number of offences and was an undischarged bankrupt who was full of confidence and very plausible.

Pascoe had placed at least £17,000 in five separate bank accounts in the name of his daughter but it was noted that the young girl 'may well lose most of the money you were setting aside for her' and that he deliberately hid the money in his daughter's name.[103]

Charles Wintersgill was sentenced to five years' imprisonment along with fines of £3,500 with Justice Cassels commenting that it was beyond his understanding how a man of Mr Wintersgill's ability and experience had yielded to temptation and that he 'must serve as an example to those who in these days occupy managerial positions'. He further admonished Mr Wintersgill saying 'It is not right that, at a time when the enemy may be almost at the gate, people who occupy such positions as you occupied should descend so low as to have no interest but their pocket.' After his sentencing Charles Wintersgill pleaded with the judge to dole out to him 'any punishment you would otherwise put upon my brothers'.[104] Speaking afterwards Detective Inspector Patterson said that although the remaining men had no previous convictions he had no hesitation in naming Charles Wintersgill as 'the brains behind the frauds'.[105]

Of the other men, Frederick Terence James was sentenced to three years' imprisonment, Thomas Wintersgill six months. Percy Lewis Stokoe and Benjamin Wintersgill were bound over for twelve months.

The case had dealt with huge sums of money and left many shocked that such people in authority in industries of great importance to the war effort were willing to engage in fraud on such a scale. So great was the interest in the case that it was extensively covered not only by the local and regional press but it also made national headlines and sparked outrage across the north-east.

In 1941, the government, anxious to restrict what it saw as unnecessary civilian travel and use of petrol and to promote healthy morale-boosting activities amongst the increasingly war-weary civilian population, introduced the 'Holidays at Home' scheme in which local authorities were encouraged to put on a variety of activities across the course of a week. Although derided in some circles the scheme proved popular in many areas of south-east Northumberland (and on Tyneside). During the August Bank Holiday week, Pegswood held its own 'Home Holidays' programme which attracted large and enthusiastic crowds. Although there were numerous events organised the majority consisted of outdoor sporting events and children's activities. The local Home Guard, ARP services and National Fire Service all took part, as did a specially invited locally based military unit along with residents from the area. With events running from Monday to Thursday, sports included: sprints and long distance races, older men's races, three-legged races, slow bicycle races, military races, ladies' races, five-a-side football competitions, tug-o-war and obstacle races.

One of the greatest attractions was the inaugural Civil Defence Cricket Competition and the final, between favourites the Ashington Control & Report Centre XI, and Hirst Park First Aid Post XI, was attended by a good crowd who witnessed an exciting match played out in a good spirit. The favourites won easily with a score of 81 for 2 compared to Hirst Park F.A.D's 75 all out.

Cricket proved a popular activity throughout the week with the second Red Cross Cricket Competition being concluded at Newbiggin during the week; again as part of a 'Holiday at Home' scheme. The competition featured eleven sides and there were several exciting matches culminating in the final, held at the miners' welfare ground, between P. Spooner's XI and R. Taylor's XI. The final saw an attendance of almost 400 which was a record for the area in recent years and a collection and raffle raised a further £12 for the Red Cross. The competition as a whole raised the sum of £44 10s.

The final itself was a low scoring but exciting one in which P. Spooner's XI won by just 4 runs, scoring 45 all out but restricting their opponents to just 41. After the final, a cup and prizes were presented by the colliery surveyor, Mr J.E. Brown, who praised the men for the spirit in which the games had been played and in raising such a sum for the Red Cross. When the Red Cross Society said that it could only provide very limited prizes the colliery officials had stepped in to provide prizes and a cup inscribed as the 'Borradale Cricket Cup'.

The Northumberland Cricket League had continued with additional teams from the services joining to take up positions vacated by those which could not continue their activities due to a lack of available members. On 8 August, Morpeth C.C. was hoping to complete the double over an RAF team (presumably from RAF Morpeth) but the absence of their two regular opening batsmen, being a man short and poor light led to a shock defeat. Batting first, the RAF team put up a seemingly achievable score of 70 with their top scorers being their opening pair (Flying Officer Curry putting on 20 and Pilot Officer Blackburn 23) while Morpeth's top bowlers were Norman

Graham and George Tait. Morpeth never got into their stride and only Stan Crozier (10), who came in at six, and N. Graham (18), coming in at seven, reaching double figures in a score of 61 all out.

We have already seen how there were increasing worries over juvenile crime and the effects of lack of parental influence (due to fathers being away in many cases) on youngsters in south-east Northumberland. Many groups existed to attempt to give youngsters some sort of focus for their energies and a range of activities. Over the August Bank Holiday several such groups were on camps in more rural parts of Northumberland and took the opportunity to hold a sports meeting at East Newtown Farm, Rothbury. The farm was being used as the camp site for twenty-three members of the Ashington Toc-H Boys' Club and they invited boys from Ashington Athletic Boys' Club and Widdrington Boys' Brigade.

Sports Held during Toc-H Boys' Club Holiday Camp at Rothbury

Event	1st Place	Runner-Up
100yds	Stan Hart (A.A.B.C.)	Derek Knox (Toc-H)
Shooting	Toc-H	A.A.B.C.
Long Jump	Stan Hart (A.A.B.C.)	Alan Sweet (Toc-H)
Quarter Mile	W. Muir (Toc-H)	James Crowther (A.A.B.C.)
Tug-o-War	Toc-H	

After the sports, the boys all sat down to teatime refreshments and in the evening a team shooting match was held using an air rifle, which saw Toc-H claim first and second places from the three teams that they entered. On the Sunday night the camp concluded with a service for the boys from Toc-H and Ashington Athletics Boys' Club at the Congregational Church, Rothbury, during which the boys were praised for their exemplary behaviour while at camp.

For the lads from Toc-H the camp was a chance to relax in rural surroundings, enjoy the fresh air, eat (eighty-six loaves of bread, thirty tins of soup, over seven gallons of milk and eight tins of condensed milk, amongst other items, were consumed). Breakfast each morning consisted of porridge cooked in a hay-box and the boys all said that this was the best porridge they had ever had! The cost of sending each boy was 15s in addition to the food ration coupons for the attendees.

Although most people have heard of the 'Dig for Victory' campaign fewer have heard of the demand for dried herbs for use in the treatment of wounds and ailments. Boy Scouts, Girl Guides, WVS, the elderly and women were all urged to go out to the hedgerows and identify and gather wild herbs. Nettles were particularly sought after as chlorophyll, used to treat wounds, could be extracted from them. In Morpeth, a factory at East Mills run by Mrs Horsborough (who was in charge of the drying room at the mill) dried herbs for medicinal use and Mrs Horsborough appealed for female volunteers in June. Other herbs collected included foxglove (used to regulate the heart beat), autumn crocus (to treat gout), valerian (a sedative), wild thyme (an antiseptic), burdock (a diuretic) and sphagnum moss (used as an absorbent sterile wound dressing).

With shortages increasing and many housewives finding it an increasing struggle to provide food for their families the government and local organisations such as the WI were constantly offering advice to the housewife on how to substitute available items for those in short supply. It was not only customers who were struggling, for shopkeepers who sold some foodstuffs, especially pastry cooks and confectioners, the shortages of products such as baking powder were a serious hindrance to their businesses and a problem for their customers. Sour milk, when combined with baking soda, provided a suitable alternative and was widely available. Some shopkeepers, such as Miss Edith Bertha Burn who was a baker and pastry cook at 42 and 44 Bridge Street, Morpeth, placed adverts in the local newspapers informing residents that they were willing to pay for contributions of sour milk.

Confectioners were also under increasing pressure from works and other emergency canteens, which had in the past sold chocolates and confectionery. In August, the Ministry of Food recognised the problem and in order to protect private retailers advised local authorities that licences to sell chocolates, sweets and confectionery should not be automatically granted to canteens unless it could be shown that there were no other outlets locally available. The Morpeth Rural Food Control Committee took this a step forward, arguing that these products were widely available at several local outlets upon the production of suitable coupons, and decided to immediately revoke all such licences held by canteens. Any canteens wishing to renew their licences were to make an application to the committee but were warned that they had from 20 August until the end of the month to make an application.

Given that many people were desperately trying to make ends meet it is no surprise that some wished to express an entrepreneurial spirit to raise funds. This led to an increase in applications to local authorities for licences to sell homemade items such as bread but these applications had to be balanced alongside the needs of already in place outlets who were, in many cases, also struggling. Morpeth Rural Food Control Committee again took this very seriously and refused the application of a Pegswood woman to sell bread from her home as there was no difficulty in obtaining bread in the area. The committee commented that it believed that licences to sell staples such as bread from private homes should be resisted and 'in no circumstances be issued'.[106]

Housewives managed to struggle on with making do but some shortages were particularly vexing with fruit being high on that list. When they believed that there were instances of unfair practices they were not slow to complain and in August there were several complaints about people being refused oranges even though they had the correct coupons. The Food Executive Officer,

Mr Primrose, said that he would personally investigate the matter and that if he discovered any wrongdoing then this would be dealt with immediately. He urged anyone who had encountered such problems to write to him.

Given the often draconian reactions to attempts to utilise the black market, hoard food, or otherwise bypass the rationing system it is very surprising that Morpeth Rural Food Control Committee agreed not to prosecute someone who had been caught altering their ration books to secure double rations of preserves. Instead the committee, under the chairmanship of Councillor J. Craigs, decided to ask the Food Executive Officer to sternly admonish the offender and to publicise the case locally to deter any future attempts at such behaviour, which, they said, would be severely dealt with.

With the demand for home-produced food the farmers of south-east Northumberland were driving themselves harder than ever. Their efforts were appreciated and the government even agreed, under certain circumstances, to relax the blackout restrictions to allow lights on tractors engaged in ploughing during the hours of darkness. The farming community, undaunted by the extra work, also helped the war effort in other ways. The Red Cross Agricultural Fund was extremely popular with the farming community throughout the war with many fundraising efforts being undertaken. In August, a charity sale was held at Morpeth Mart. Organised by the Morpeth and Bedlington branches of

The Mayor of Morpeth auctions of a patriotic donkey in aid of charity. (The Journal)

the National Farmers' Union (NFU) and the Tritlington Young Farmers' Club, the event culminated in a sale with the mayor of Morpeth as auctioneer and one of the lots being a donkey draped, of course, with the Union Jack.

Towards the end of August the Northumberland Home Guard was struck by scandal when one of its battalion commanders was tried at a court martial accused of having fraudulently acquired over £200 from Home Guard funds. Lieutenant Colonel A.J. Williams of Milbank Crescent, Bedlington, was the headmaster of Bedlington Secondary School as well as an officer in the Home Guard. He had taken the funds as he was in personal financial difficulty, had obtained money from a money lender and did not wish his wife to find out about his problems. After being found guilty Lieutenant Colonel Williams was cashiered (ritually dismissed from the service) and sentenced to one year with hard labour (although six months of this was remitted by the king). During his four-day long court martial he had at first attempted to deny the authority of the hearing, saying that he was not a regular serving officer. He had then attempted to say that the situation was a result of his having to entertain visiting officers and the confusion caused by the rapid expansion of the Home Guard at the time. Williams faced a heavy additional penalty as he would lose his £800 per annum wage as well as the £300 per year pension which he would have been entitled to in a year's time (he had been headmaster for seventeen years).

The combination of blackout, fewer police, men being away on service, the presence of many strangers (especially soldiers) in the area and a perceived lapse in morale standards combined to lead to an increase in the number of women who found themselves prosecuted for offences such as larceny, which was often linked to suspected or proven prostitution. In November, the magistrates at Morpeth heard the case of Mrs Hannah Burns (29) who was accused of having stolen £4 10s from a man whom she had lured to Castle Wood. The bench heard how the accused had been in several public houses and had drunk several beers along with port before going with two unknown women to a snack bar in the Market Place for food. Here she engaged a man at another table in conversation before agreeing to meet him outside. The victim stated that he had agreed to go into the wood with the woman, with the bench agreeing that he had placed himself in a 'very precarious position' by agreeing to the woman's proposal (hinting very strongly that prostitution was the reason for this invitation). The defendant, however, stated that the man had offered to buy her a whisky and to give her £1 but first to go for a walk in the woods. Entering the woods at approximately 6.00 pm the couple walked to a secluded spot before the man caught the accused with her hand in his coat pocket. The alleged victim grabbed the woman's wrist and she screamed. Two local men, Richard Robert Ashworth Dixon and Stanley Thistlethwaite, who were returning home, heard the screams and investigated. They came upon the couple and upon examining them found that the woman had several receipts and documents belonging to the alleged victim in her hand. The man said that she had stolen the sum of money from him and then asked the men to accompany them to the police station. As they walked through the woods Mr Thistlethwaite observed the accused rummaging in her dress before surreptitiously dropping several items which proved to be papers belonging to the man. Giving evidence, Police Sergeant Turnbull said that upon searching the woman the police matron found the sum of £1 4s 6d. While at the station the accused told Sergeant Turnbull of the offered whisky and said that the man had shown her some papers which she had hung onto as a guarantee of the promised payment of £1. The bench, stating that such a prosecution 'might be the means of stopping a very dangerous habit',[107] took little time in finding Mrs Burns guilty of the lesser charge of attempted larceny and sentenced her to one month in prison.

Throughout the year, casualties continued to mount. As well as from all branches of the armed forces there were a great many from the Merchant Navy. In July, a telegram arrived for Miss K. Douglas at Coquet Cottage, Oldgate Street, Morpeth, informing her of the loss at sea of her brother Robert Darling Douglas. Aged 52, Robert had lived in Morpeth since the age of 5 (he was born at Alnwick) and had served his apprenticeship at Swinney Bros. Ltd before joining the Merchant Navy in 1912 and rising through the ranks to the position of Chief Engineer. He had served in this position aboard the US owned ship *San Blas* of the United Fruit Company. Although owned by a US firm the *San Blas* sailed under the British flag (some sources say Panamanian) and was torpedoed and sunk shortly before 10.00 pm on 16 June by *U-158* while en route from Galveston to Puerto Barrios, Guatemala. The torpedo blew the stern to pieces and the ship sunk in four minutes with no chance to launch lifeboats. Of the forty-four man crew (thirty-nine merchant seamen and five US navy personnel) only fourteen survived (twelve merchantmen and two naval personnel) by clinging to rafts for thirteen days before being rescued.[108]

We have already seen how the people of south-east Northumberland gave generously to wartime charities. It was not only in money or comforts that sacrifices were made for the war effort. With the conflict raging across the world, donations of blood were all important and across the area the men and women of the Tyneside Blood Transfusion Service worked in both Tyneside and Northumberland. In July, the service set up in one of the main shopping streets of Whitley Bay with the crew of an American service ambulance. They quickly attracted a large crowd of volunteers who, after being tested by the American and British personnel, were registered as donors. It was through such efforts that many ordinary people found they could actively contribute to the war effort.

With food rationing and ever-worsening shortages a great many south-east Northumbrians were finding it increasingly difficult to make ends

Shoppers queue to donate blood in Whitley Bay. (The Daily Mirror)

meet. For these people the local emergency feeding centres (for use after air raids) and British Restaurants were a vital source of cheap, nourishing food. However, the newly opened British Restaurant at Blyth quickly ran into controversy in the spring of 1942 and was roundly criticised by the local council. The sub-committee which ran the restaurant resented the criticism of their colleagues and put forward their mass resignation along with a motion stating that the censure of their colleagues had been an 'unwarranted attack'. The council reacted furiously and had this motion rejected and removed from the minutes, although they accepted the resignations. The allegations centred around claims by townspeople of preferential treatment for members of the National Fire Service, and Councillor Heatley claimed that at one emergency feeding station he had witnessed townspeople being refused soup while 'other persons [i.e. firemen] who had certain tickets in their pockets received "beautiful plates" of soup'. The chair of the sub-committee, Alderman J. Reilly, replied that the problem had lasted only two days, if it existed at all, and that the firemen had been told by others in the queue to go into the restaurant ahead of the townspeople. Reilly was prevented from replying to Councillor Heatley when he was ruled out of order by the Deputy Mayor, Alderman A. Walton. The deputy mayor had earlier described the motion put forward as extremely arrogant and had urged other councillors to vote to remove the minute saying that it was 'a supercilious form of resolution'.[109]

The approach of the fourth wartime Christmas saw a more muted response as war-weariness and increasing shortages led to a more sombre mood. Across the area the holidays were celebrated in a relatively quiet fashion with church services being well attended and the long weekend providing some welcome relief for hard-pushed workers. Despite the perceived quietness there were happy scenes in some houses where members of the services were lucky enough to be on leave and dances and carol services were well attended. A dance held on Boxing Night at Morpeth Parochial Hall attracted a large and festive crowd who were keen to dance to the musical accomplishment of Billy McCarthy's Band.

Toys, especially modern, mechanical, ones, were in very short supply and many families made do with smaller gifts and homemade items. Many fathers who had a talent for handicrafts rose to the occasion and in Ashington it was commented upon that there were more homemade toys on show than ever before, with model aircraft being particularly popular. Confectionery was also in short supply and many without children sacrificed their sweet ration to provide for little ones: the Ashington Home Guard donated 300 bars of chocolate to a local children's party. Under the leadership of Major J. Abercrombie, MBE, MM, the men of the Home Guard held the successful party at the Trade Union Hall on Boxing Day. As a further bonus the members of the Home Guard and their adult relatives also gave the children 3d each and the children enjoyed a tea party followed by games and a concert. During the evening the Home Guardsmen's wives were treated to a social evening with music supplied by the Home Guard band.

The forty-two annuitants of the various funds held in trust by Morpeth Corporation were given their annual gift of a load of coal and a joint of beef. The child occupants of the Cottage Homes at Bowmer Bank and High Stanners (Morpeth) were treated to a Christmas tree along with gifts provided by the Youth Guild. At the Thomas Taylor Homes in Netherton the elderly occupants were treated to a Christmas lunch of pork, beef, rabbit and vegetables by the poor law union of Morpeth. The tables of the homes were decorated with artificial sweet peas and a cheerful speech was given by Mr Edward Stanley, the relieving officer for Morpeth who had not missed the Christmas lunch event for thirty-one years.

Sports were also popular, with football, rugby and dog racing events all being held and well supported during the holidays. At Morpeth Grammar School the annual rugby match between the school team and an old boys' XV was held. In what was described a very even and entertaining match played in wet conditions the old boys ran out winners by the score of 11-3. Elsewhere, football matches were organised between local organisations such as that between Ashington Squadron ATC and Sunderland Wing ATC at Ashington at Portland Park.

CHAPTER 5

1943: Onslaught

As the fifth year of the war began there were signs that people in south-east Northumberland remained keen to wring what enjoyment they could from their restricted free time. In Morpeth the first week of 1943 saw the town's two picture houses do a roaring trade with the Coliseum, in particular, experiencing crowded houses to enjoy the musical film *Wake Up and Dream* (1942, originally titled *What's Cookin* when released in the US in 1942) starring The Andrews Sisters, Gloria Jean and Robert Paige. There was a definite flavour of escapism in two of the most popular features with large crowds watching another musical; this time the attraction was *My Gal Sal* (1942) starring Rita Hayworth and Victor Mature. Clearly the majority of people wanted to escape the rigours, worries and boredom which accompanied life in wartime Britain. However, at least one feature at the Coliseum (colloquially known as 'The Colly' to Morpethians) was of a tenser nature. This was *Saboteur* (1942), an Alfred Hitchcock thriller about a man who goes on the run after being wrongfully accused of sabotaging the aircraft factory where he worked, and starring Priscilla Lane and Robert Cummings. By the end of the week, however, 'The Colly' had reverted to another piece of escapism with the comedy musical *Sleepytime Gal* (1942) starring Judy Canova.[110]

The children of Morpeth were treated to a New Year's party by the long-established Corporal and Privates' Dance Committee (made up of men from military units stationed in the town) at the YMCA (the committee had for some time organised dances at the YMCA and the Parochial Hall to raise funds for war charities). The dance was to take place on Saturday, 2 January starting at 2.00 pm but such was the popularity of past entertainments laid on by the committee that a large crowd of guests from the local schools were assembled well before that time. By the time the hall was opened to the guests the crowd was estimated to number approximately 120. Music was provided by the locally based Argyll & Sutherland Highlanders' Tam-O'-Shanter Concert Party while magician Jack Britton also proved a great hit with the youngsters. Food was also provided and there were many games and competitions to be taken part in. The winners of a variety of games were awarded prizes by Captain Gloyne. The prize-winners included: Andrew Nicolle, Ken Farthing, Victor Scott, R. Burton, Veronica Scott, Olive Elliott, Margaret Scott and Jean Elliott.

The 'Ashington Widow' writing in the *Morpeth Herald* continued 1943 in the same vein as previously in the war by commenting pithily on the lack of appreciation for culture in the mining communities of the area. On the first day of the year she described how a troupe of government sponsored actors had been left thoroughly dejected by the miniscule turnout from the miners to see the 'highbrow' plays that they performed during the week, including classics by Shakespeare, Shaw, etc. The manager and director of the Market Theatre Players, Richard Wordsworth, asked dejectedly how they could attract the miners to their performances, only to be told by the correspondent that she could offer no advice as it was a persistent problem in the area although, apparently, the Durham miners turned out in large numbers when the troupe passed through that county.

The widow went on to suggest a certain ignorance amongst the miners saying that they had only nine dominating interests, these being 'work, working conditions, wages, food, sleep, dog racing, beer, gardening and the cinema'. This, of course, quite fails to appreciate the working hours and the conditions that the miners were experiencing. It was only natural that these men would prefer to spend their Saturdays resting or finding some form of enjoyment rather than attending theatre performances: gardening was positively encouraged as a huge contribution to the war effort. The widow's opinion was that any attempt to engage the miners with high culture was simply the result of 'wishful thinking' on the part of those who thought the miners were ready for culture.[111] While decrying this attitude the widow explained that such neglect would lead to the town being blacklisted in the future for such ventures but was forced to admit that few would care.

We have already seen how, in 1941, the members of Broomhill Cycling Club continued with their usual programme of events as far as was possible. This attempt to maintain an attempt at normality continued throughout 1943 with the club continuing to meet on Sundays. On 3 January the members set off on a lengthy route which took in Chevington Moor, Causey Park, Longhorsley Moor (where the party had an alfresco lunch). Following this they set off for Stanton, Pigdon, Benridge and Mitford (where they enjoyed a cup of tea). As night was now setting in the club members set off for home via Hebron, Ulgham and Widdrington.

Minor crimes continued to be harshly punished especially when they involved habitual criminal activity. The Moothall magistrates heard two such cases on the last day of 1942. The first involved the theft and destruction of several glasses from the Clousden Hill Inn at Forest Hall by three youths. One of these youths, George William Keith Storey (19) was described as a habitual troublemaker who had three previous convictions. Storey told the magistrates that he was now in gainful employment and promised to behave better in the future and was fined the sum of 20s. His co-accused, Robert Hingley (17) and William McKenzie Carr (19), were also found guilty and fined 15s and 20s respectively. The second case involved the theft of 112lbs of coal from his place of employment at the Isabella Pit, Blyth. The accused, William Walker (42), was described as being 'a persistent coal thief since 1925, having been convicted of this offence six times'.[112]

A particularly tragic case at Newbiggin highlighted the tragedies of service life separating families from one another. Private Austin Corless (38) of the Pioneer Corps was charged at Ashington Police Court with having stabbed to death his 5-year-old son, attempting to murder his wife Violet and attempting to kill himself. Corless maintained that he was not guilty and the case was subsequently heard at the assizes in Newcastle in early February. The case lasted all day and the bench and jury heard the tragic tale of a devoted father and husband who had been driven to murder by an unfaithful spouse. During his time on remand at Durham, Corless wrote to his commanding officer stating that his wife had caused him 'great trouble' as she had wanted a divorce after being unfaithful to him with an RAF man who had given her a ring. Corless also admitted that he had wanted to 'take the boy [his son] with him, that he loved the boy, and that he lost his reason'.[113]

Violet Corless, who had been seriously wounded during the attack, confessed on the stand that she had indeed experienced trouble in her marriage and that she 'admitted familiarity on one occasion' with the RAF man and that she had caused her husband many sleepless nights with her behaviour.[114]

His representative said of his client that 'the whole of the life of Corless was centred in his affection for his wife, his home, his two children and also the illegitimate child of his wife' and that he 'might be described as a too loving and too forgiving husband'.[115] He had written to his wife prior to his return home to say that he was relieved that she was going to send the RAF man's ring back and that 'she had come to her senses and would not see "the swine again"'. In the same letter Corless also confessed to Violet that he 'adored the ground she walked on'.[116] It emerged during the trial that Corless's brother had died in a mental hospital 28 years before but that Corless himself had shown no sign of mental instability. His lawyer, however, argued that Corless was indeed guilty but insane and based a large part of his defence on the argument that only insanity would have provoked Corless to murder the child he loved so much. Indeed, Corless had confessed upon his arrest that his son 'was a little hero in my arms' but that his wife (and un-named others) had 'drove me crazy that day, and I lost my reason'.[117]

Despite the evidence from the doctor at Durham Prison that he had found no evidence of insanity or clinical depression Corless's lawyer still petitioned the jury for a guilty but insane verdict. In his closing statements Mr Justice Birkett told the jury that the whole case depended on them reaching a decision on whether they believed that Corless was, at the time of the offences, out of his mind due to the stress which he was under. The jury took just 45 minutes to return with a verdict of guilty but insane and Corless was detained at His Majesty's pleasure.

As we have previously seen, the shortages of foods could prove a temptation to some to embark on criminal endeavours. In the first week of the year, Morpeth magistrates heard an odd case involving the theft of 157lbs of Brussels sprouts from the market garden of George Charlton (Jun.) at 7 Fenwick Grove, Morpeth. The sprouts, obviously in demand through December, were stolen by an employee of Messrs Charlton named Thomas Morgan. Mr Morgan, of 9 Dacre Court, Morpeth, admitted the theft to police. Mr Morgan had been taking the sprouts in batches from his place of work to his mother, Sarah Jane Scott, in Stobhill Gate and she had been selling them to a local shop for 10s per 12lbs. This had been going on for some time and one of the owners of the market garden, Jack Charlton, stated to the bench that the firm were not being vindictive and wished to continue employing Mr Morgan and that they allowed their employees to take home three or four pounds of vegetables for their own use if asked but the employees knew that they were not permitted to sell these on. Mr Charlton estimated the sprouts to be worth £2 12s 4d and said that the practice of allowing staff to dig up veg was open to abuse during hours of darkness and might have to be, reluctantly, stopped. The bench convicted Mr Morgan and seem to have taken a very dim view of the theft ordering him to pay the sum of £3 10s within the month or go to prison for one month.

It was not only foodstuffs which were in demand. With the growing numbers of people raising pigs and hens there was an increased demand for feed, which could often prove a temptation to theft. In October a 50-year-old labourer from Silverhill Cottages, Seaton Delaval, pleaded guilty to stealing a quantity of wheat from the barn of Hedley West Farm. Thomas Corrigan stated in his confession that he had stolen the wheat in order to feed his hens but he denied that it had been stolen from inside the barn. He was fined £2.

Some of the offences for which otherwise ordinary members of the community were criminalised seem to have been remarkably trivial. In October, there was an example at Morpeth of relatively minor food regulations leading to a prosecution. Janet Shell of Gallow Hill Farm, Cambo, was caught by the Ministry of Food Enforcement Officer for the district, Mr J.A.T. Wright, who described how he had been standing in a shop door at New Market when he saw the accused enter the library shop carrying a basket. After following and confronting the accused he ascertained that there were several small parcels of eggs in the basket with each egg being marked with an H in pencil. Mr Wright loaned Shell an indelible pencil to re-mark the eggs which she said were being sold to hatch on.

The next day Mr Wright visited Shell at her home to enquire as to what had become of the eggs and was told that she had sold them to two separate women whose husbands ran a poultry farm. She claimed that she had never heard of the regulation which said that she had to obtain written evidence from the purchasers that the eggs were to be hatched on and could not name them, nor was she aware that the eggs should have been marked with a red H. The accused voluntarily said that she had been selling eggs for hatching since 1942 and had never encountered any such problems before. Shell's defence claimed that without proof of the purchase there was no case to answer and that Mrs Shell had done what she was thought adequate to adhere to the law and also that the matter of how the eggs should have been marked seemed to be very unclear; even to the Ministry of Food official. The bench obviously thought the matter a relatively trivial one but still returned a guilty verdict fining Mrs Shell 5s.

The same sitting heard a case of the overselling of tomatoes by Seabrook Bros., a firm of nurserymen at Mitford Road Nurseries. The firm had a small shop at 2 Oldgate in Morpeth from which it sold its produce. The Ministry of Food claimed that it had sold 22lbs in excess of their quote of tomatoes. The Ministry argued that the order giving growers a regular quota was promulgated in order to ensure a fair distribution of items of produce for all members of the public. The excess tomatoes would have gone into a local pool for equitable distribution and Seabrook Bros. would have been paid 6d per lb. The Ministry confirmed that there was no allegation of profiteering against the firm while the firm claimed that it had simply been an oversight on its part. The bench imposed a fine of £10 with a further two guineas in costs (just over £500 today).

We have already seen how the sacrifices made by the airmen of RAF Bomber Command were appreciated by the people of the area. Many who had completed a tour of operations lost their lives in flying accidents, while training others, or signed on for a second tour and been subsequently killed. Pilot Officer Albert Edward Gray was a 22-year-old wireless operator/air gunner from Whitley Bay. He had flown his first tour in 1941 with 83 Squadron completing thirty-two operations including two to Berlin. On one operation he and his crew had sunk a 7,000 ton enemy ship off the Frisian Isles while on another occasion the navigator's equipment had been lost due to enemy action and the then Sergeant Gray had been responsible for navigating the aircraft home using his visual loop indicator. He had enjoyed a high reputation and had been important in helping to instruct new wireless operators on the squadron. For his actions Sergeant Gray was awarded the DFM in October 1941. By June 1943, he was assigned to 515 Squadron which was engaged on highly secret operations to attempt to jam German radar. The squadron was equipped with the obsolete Boulton-Paul Defiant as an interim measure. On 8 June, Pilot Officer Gray was flying in Defiant II (AA435) when the pilot (Flight Sergeant Steel) became disoriented in foggy conditions and crashed into the cliffs at Beachy Head, killing both himself and Pilot Officer Gray. Pilot Officer Gray is buried in Hartley (South) Cemetery, Whitley Bay, where his headstone bears the poignant inscription:

> 'We sing his songs
> And miss his love.
> Now he is safe
> With God above.
> Dad and all.'[118]

We have already seen how local shipyards could provide opportunities for criminal activities and the familiar name of Blyth Shipbuilding & Dry Docks Company once again made the headlines when two directors of the firm were charged (in conjunction with the already imprisoned Charles Wintersgill) with conspiracy and bribery to win contracts dating from 1935 to March 1943 and several counts of defrauding the Admiralty. The case made national headlines as the two men, Sir Arthur Munro Sutherland (76) and Alderman Robert Stanley Dalgliesh (71), were also former lord mayors of Newcastle while Sir Arthur was also at the time the High Sheriff of Northumberland. Amongst the accused was an Admiralty official named Charles James Butt, who was alleged to have been the party to receive the bribes. The two directors were charged with having illegally paid £155 (almost £6,500) to Butt while Butt was also charged under the Official Secrets Act with having communicated the details of future terms for Admiralty minesweeper tenders. Although the accused were originally charged at Blyth in March, because of the positions held in north-east society by several of the accused the case was heard at Leeds, beginning in July. Both Sir Arthur and Alderman Dalgliesh denied the charges against them with Sir Arthur being particularly vehement in his denials saying that 'He cannot conceive what grounds there are for these allegations against him' and that he 'has a most complete defence to these charges and he wants to make it quite clear that this slur on his name should be removed'.[119]

The original evidence for the case had come from Charles Wintersgill who, while in prison, had informed the police that in 1935 he had, under instruction, visited Mr Butt at his Newcastle office, where he was Admiralty Superintendent of Warship Production on the North East Coast, with a view to solicit Admiralty orders for the yard. At the meeting he alleged that Mr Butt said that if he was to take part in such a scheme he should be recognised for his contribution. Wintersgill claimed that he conferred with Alderman Dalgliesh who gave his approval and that from that time until 1940 Mr Butt had received £50 (£2,092) for every ship subsequently ordered from the yard. After 1940 a different arrangement had been put in place whereby Mr Butt was paid £25 per ship until March 1942 and that over that time he had been paid the sum of £1,750 (over £73,000 today).Wintersgill alleged that Alderman Dalgliesh had been the man behind the scheme. Sir Arthur had no knowledge of it at the time but after discovering it had done nothing to halt it. Wintersgill also outlined how he had always been the one responsible for paying Mr Butt in £1 notes which had been entered into the company petty cash accounts as being for 'special services'.[120]

After being brought from Durham Prison, Wintersgill alleged that Butt had become even more use to the company when he was promoted and appointed as superintendent of labour and materials at Admiralty HQ. He described how the yard had been asked to tender for two minesweepers and had submitted a tender of £61,250 apiece. Butt then gave information on the other tenders which had been submitted and they realised that their quote was £11,000 per vessel below their nearest rival. Having seen this information the directors sent a letter to the Admiralty stating that the figure 1 should have been a 7. This still meant that they undercut their rivals but also that they were able to gain an extra £12,000 on the order.

Sir Patrick Hastings, the lawyer representing Sir Arthur, unsuccessfully moved to have the charges against his client dismissed as he claimed there was no evidence against him, and on 23 July Sir Arthur took to the witness box. He argued that the only evidence against him came from Wintersgill and hinted that this might be the result of ill-feeling after Wintersgill had been imprisoned the previous year. Sir Arthur then went on to say that he knew very little of the goings on at Blyth as he viewed the company as 'a bit of a side line'. He stated that he had only become involved with the company after the previous company there went bankrupt, a fact he described as being 'disastrous to the people of the town', and portrayed his involvement as a charitable act 'with a view to restoring prosperity to Blyth'.[121] Sir Arthur then confirmed that he had been unaware that Wintersgill had been stealing from the company but admitted that he had met Mr Butt on several former occasions and that he had once visited his country home. Sir Arthur denied that he had ever known about the money being paid to Mr Butt and that he had placed great faith in Mr Wintersgill.

Sir Arthur then said that after Wintersgill's arrest he had heard rumours of an altered tender and had asked the yard manager to enquire. Upon being told that a tender had been altered he had been reassured that the Admiralty had been informed as to the reason for this and was satisfied. When confronted with the evidence of twenty-one receipts of payment which included payments to Mr Butt Sir Arthur said that he had been 'very much shocked to see Butt's name on them, and I thought surely Wintersgill had not been bribing a man in Butt's position'.

Sir Arthur then alleged that on 22 June Mr Wintersgill's brother Benjamin had visited him and demanded that he buy Wintersgill's shares for £2 10s per share instead of the £1 he had offered and that his brother would also share information that would enable him to evade the charges which had been proffered against him. After hearing this Sir Arthur said that he threw Benjamin Wintersgill out of his home.

Under cross-examination Sir Arthur again said that the yard was a side line but admitted that he owned 99 per cent of the shares and that most of the profits were his. He also admitted that, after the death of Lord Runciman, the other director in 1937, both he and Alderman Dalgliesh had been willing to sell the yard if a decent offer had been made for it. Sir Arthur was also forced to admit that after seeing the receipts he had formed the impression that perhaps Wintersgill had been bribing Mr Butt but could not believe it of either man and had not made any attempt to investigate or allay his suspicions beyond speaking to Alderman Dalgliesh, who told him he knew nothing of it. Sir Arthur also admitted that he had 'never looked at the books and was very seldom at the yard' and that neither Wintersgill nor Alderman Dalgliesh had told him the altered tender would fraudulently raise a further £12,000 for the yard.

Alderman Dalgliesh was still maintaining that he was too ill to take the stand but despite doctor's certificates the judge ordered that he be examined by doctors for each party and that it was up to the jury to decide whether or not Dalgliesh was fit enough or not to take the stand. It was subsequently decided that Alderman Dalgliesh was not fit enough to take the stand. Both defences were keen to make the point that their clients were respected men who had become involved with the yard in order to benefit the people of Blyth and that neither man had taken a great interest in the running of the yard, entrusting this to Wintersgill. Equally, both defence teams were keen to try to further blacken the name of Mr Wintersgill and to portray him as the sole wrong-doer in the case. The lawyer representing Mr Butt said that only his client and Mr Wintersgill knew whether or not money had actually changed hands but he stated his client's previous good character and his service to the Admiralty and made the allegation that Mr Wintersgill could easily have entered these payments into the books but 'put the money in his own pocket'.[122]

After five days the trial concluded. Sir Arthur Munro Sutherland was found not guilty on all charges and was discharged immediately. Both Alderman Dalgliesh and Mr Butt, however, were found guilty of all charges offered against them. Dalgliesh was sentenced to fifteen months' imprisonment (in the Second Division), ordered to pay a total of £2,500 in fines and £1,500 costs (combined, more than £167,000 today).[123] In sentencing Dalgliesh Mr Justice Tucker said that but for Dalgliesh's age and medical condition 'the punishment would be much more severe'. Butt was sentenced to three years' penal imprisonment with a further eighteen months to run concurrently. Addressing Butt Mr Justice Tucker said that he was 'a younger man employed in his Majesty's service, which you have grievously betrayed'. It was noted in the press that before leaving the court Sir Arthur had shaken hands with both Alderman Dalgliesh and Mr Butt leaving the impression that he still believed that the blame was solely attached to Mr Wintersgill.[124]

The crime involving the yard did not end there. In October, a driver, Cuthbert Gallacher (31), was found guilty of having stolen a large quantity of timber, scrap metal, brass, iron and two shovels from the shipyard. The defendant had even built a shed from some of the timber, which he used to store the materials which were valued at over £15 (over £600 today). Despite the fact that Mr Gallacher had not made any profit from the theft and pleaded poverty the bench sentenced him to three months' prison with hard labour.

Two men were knocked down and injured on 26 August, when a horse-drawn lorry owned by the Co-operative society went out of control at Cambois ferry. The driver, Mr Joseph Hepworth, described how the horse had spooked and run out of control down the steep road towards the ferry. Two men, William Wilson (42) of 7 Gees Houses, Cambois, and William Edwards of 3 Gas Row, Cowpen Colliery, were standing on the ferry talking when they saw the horse and cart coming towards them at speed. Although they tried to take avoiding action, they were both struck and knocked to the ground. The horse and cart together with Mr Hepworth crashed through a barrier before falling into the river, which was approximately 30ft deep at that point. Mr Hepworth got into difficulties but Mr Wilson, despite having a badly bruised and swollen leg, got up from the ground and dived into the water to rescue him. For his actions Mr Wilson was awarded a certificate, along with 15 guineas, by the Humane Society.

Having already seen how ordinary people could be criminalised by wartime laws and how the shift in the economy caused by shortages and rationing could lead to some being tempted by the possibility of large profits it comes as no surprise to see that cases continued throughout the year. In September, a special sitting of the magistrates at Morpeth heard a case involving the illegal auction sale of furniture which involved ninety-nine separate summonses and two well-known local businessmen. The defendants were Mr Thomas Bertram Waters, an auctioneer who traded as Thomas Waters & Son at the Borough Hall Sales Rooms at Wellway, and Mr William R. Whittle, who owned a furniture removals business at 28 Hood Street. In a financially complex case it was alleged that in May and June the two men had knowingly sold furniture that was not owned by Mr Whittle at the Borough Hall Sales Rooms and which had been obtained by him solely with the view to making a profit. At the time furniture was in short supply and recently enacted laws had forced both seller and auctioneer to have a licence to sell the furniture, which could only be the personal property of the seller and not part of any business stock, with strict records being kept. This was to stop the early war practice of selling furniture at auction where it fetched far higher prices than normal due to the shortages.

Board of Trade inspectors had seen evidence of many transactions between the two men, which had not been in line with the new regulations and to highlight the profitability of such a scheme they gave evidence of one item of furniture tripling in price after being bought for £41 and sold at auction for £130 with a suite being bought for £28 and sold for £62 10s. The Board of Trade alleged that furniture had been purchased for £1,678 and subsequently sold for £2,410 with a net profit after deductions of approximately £731 (over £30,000 today) although, taking into account commission of 5 per cent, this would increase to approximately £850 profit (over £35,500). The defendants acknowledged their guilt but queried the amounts concerned claiming that they had in fact only made a profit of approximately £650 (just over £27,000) and this sum should be further reduced for transport of the furniture and travelling expenses (the furniture had been bought at Newcastle and Whitley Bay).

The defence also made much of the previous good character of the two defendants and that Mr Waters, in particular, was well-known to the bench as a successful local businessman of some standing who had been actively involved in public affairs. The defendants' solicitor summed up by adding that although there had been ninety-nine summonses these covered only twenty-three transactions and he hoped that the bench would also take into account the fact that this matter had been hanging over the two men for some months. The magistrates retired to consult in private before emerging to declare that the two men had pleaded guilty to very serious charges, fining Mr Waters the total sum of £928 15s (almost £39,000) and Mr Whittle the sum of £291 5s (over £12,000).

Although the traditional heavy industries of mining, shipbuilding and engineering were experiencing a wartime boom period it was clear to many politicians that such industries would once again contract when the war was, hopefully, won and, showing a positive spirit, the Mayor of Blyth, Alderman A. Walton, asked several local authorities to a meeting to be held in the New Year at Blyth to discuss the possibilities of attracting and developing light industries in the area. The mayor had been motivated to act by a recent conference organised by Lord Ridley at Newcastle, which had discussed the theme of post-war industrial aid on the north-east coast. Drawing on the post-First World War experiences of Blyth Council the mayor knew that fishing and pottery industries had been investigated but nothing had come of this.

There were also far more pressing industrial worries with shortages of coal beginning to have an impact on wartime industry. This was of grave concern to the government and it was estimated that an additional 700,000 mine workers were needed throughout the country to increase supply to an acceptable level. With this in mind, schemes were begun to move physically fit surface workers into underground operations. This move, which affected all of those aged 18-25, was often resented and in May five such men were brought before the court at Blyth charged with refusing official directions moving them to underground work. The first four cases to be heard were all from Horton Grange Colliery and all were employed as haulage workers. James Ellis (19) argued that it was unfair 'for a person to be forced down the pit' to which the somewhat pompous prosecutor replied that it was 'a jolly sight better to be told to go down the pit than to face machine guns'. An unsympathetic bench found Ellis guilty and ordered him down the pit and fined him the sum of £3 which had to be paid in a month or the choice of serving one month in prison.

Next it was the turn of Aubrey Rutherford (18). Mr Rutherford again argued that he believed it was unfair to force someone to go down the pit against their will and added that there was no future career prospects in such a job. He related how he had tried to volunteer but was told at the time that he was in a reserved occupation. Mr Rutherford bluntly told the bench that he would far rather 'go into the fighting forces' but this cut no ice and, once more, the defendant was fined the same sum as his co-worker. The next two cases were those of George Ferguson (18) and Archibald Summers (23) who were given identical punishments.

The final case was that of Blyth man, James Whiteman, who instead of proclaiming the unfairness of the action claimed that he was afraid of confined spaces. Whiteman also informed the magistrates that he had tried to volunteer for RAF aircrew duties but had failed the mathematics exam and that he had since volunteered for other military duties. The magistrates suspended the case for a fortnight while medical opinions were sought. However, it seems most unlikely that Mr Whiteman did suffer from a severe fear of confined spaces as he could hardly have wished to serve in the cramped confines of an aircraft (most likely, given his background, a cramped air gunner's turret in an RAF bomber).

Although the activities of the Civil Defence Services had fallen off somewhat as the number of enemy air raids slackened, the local authorities (and the services themselves) were keen to ensure the maintenance of both morale and vigilance. The men and women of the local services were treated to a rather pompous and overblown lecture by London's Regional Commissioner, Admiral Sir Edward Evans, at Wallington. Admiral Evans began by stating that the country had 'got rid of the old blimps, those mouldy old blighters' but foresaw the rise of another danger to the war effort claiming that 'another fungus has grown up in this country – "the twirps"'. Admiral Evan placed the 'twirps' into two categories, temporary and permanent. The temporary 'twirps', he claimed, were those who thought only of themselves and who caused strikes and so on, while the permanent 'twirps' were those in authority who produced lengthy circulars thinking that 'victory will be won by fighting a paper and office war'.[125]

One of the ways in which people were encouraged to feel a part of the war effort was the adoption of a particular ship or aircraft. The port town of Blyth, for example, keenly followed the exploits of the minesweeper HMS *Blyth* and in 1942 agreed to formally adopt the ship. This resulted in a visit in February by the captain of HMS *Blyth* who presented a plaque to the mayor commemorating the event. Commander Oddy expressed his thanks to the townspeople for their frequent gifts to the men under his command and commented on how he had seen many pretty girls about the town and suggested that they could perhaps write to 'a lonely sailor'. The minesweeper had already led an adventurous war with two former commanding officers being awarded the DSO while captaining the vessel. Commander Oddy could relate how, while under Commander Eade, DSO, HMS *Blyth* had participated in the Dieppe Raid, leading a group of minesweepers.

As we have seen previously, RAF Morpeth suffered at times from a particularly chaotic level of organisation with the lack of adequate flying control facilities and the (frustration-fuelled) indiscipline of many of the Polish aircrew who persisted in making low level passes over a number of communities in south-east Northumberland. On 29 March there was yet another fatal incident at the airfield which this time seems to have been the result of pomposity and poor weather. On that day a visiting Air Vice Marshall from 29 Group insisted upon a flying display by several of the unit's widely despised Blackburn Bothas. Ordinary gunnery sorties had been cancelled due to low cloud and visibility but for some reason the air show was pressed on with. After giving a brief display, two of the aircraft attempted to land at the same time (again highlighting the poor control over the airfield) and collided at approximately 1,000ft. Both aircraft crashed 2 miles east of Morpeth and all nine aircrew were killed; one after suffering a parachute malfunction after bailing out at low level. Amongst the dead was the most senior Polish pilot in the unit, Major Stanislaw Zygmunt Zarski (46). Demonstrating the international nature of the RAF, and RAF Morpeth in particular, the dead included five Dutchmen (all members of the Royal Netherlands Navy Air Service), a British Leading Aircraftman and the New Zealand pilot of the other Botha, Pilot Officer George Rowan Jackson (22).[126]

RAF Morpeth became a minor part of RAF history when on 6 April two WAAF flight mechanics were posted to the station. They were the first ever women to be employed in this trade by the service and were obviously a success as, by June, a trade training base was established at Morpeth to retrain former balloon operators in the WAAF as flight mechanics, thus freeing up more men for service.

RAF Morpeth was home to a large variety of aircraft types and in the summer this was added to when a flight of Auster Aerial Observation Post (AOP) Mk III spotter planes arrived. The units consisted of A Flight from 652 Squadron and was based at Morpeth while it flew artillery observation practice flights to the ranges at Otterburn. The aircrew were largely army personnel although the maintenance of the aircraft was the responsibility of the RAF.[127]

Finally, in June, the hated Bothas began to be replaced by the Avro Anson which, although not able to hold as many trainee gunners as the Botha, was a far more reliable aircraft with a much better safety and serviceability record. Although this was a very welcome development it was a slow process and there was still time for two more fatal crashes involving Bothas. The first happened on 9 June when a Botha piloted by another Pole, Podporucznik (equivalent to Second Lieutenant) Zaleski, crashed in the grounds of the mental hospital at nearby Stannington killing all on board. The cause of the crash was said to have been an engine failure; common enough with the maligned Botha. Towards the end of the month yet another Polish pilot and his crew were killed when their Botha stalled and crashed on the runway at Morpeth after aborting an attempted landing. The pilot, Podporucznik Ryszard Resko, was buried at Morpeth (St Mary's) Churchyard alongside one of his three-man crew, Leading Aircraftman Harold Victor Logan (18) of Castlethorpe, Lincolnshire. They joined six of those killed in the crash of 29 March and Kapral (Corporal) Stefan Zawilinski of the Polish Air Force (killed on 10 May) and American Flying Officer Allen Theodore Lewis Rossignol (31), RAFVR, who had been killed on 2 June.[128]

As the year progressed, training at Morpeth reached new heights with the station producing its 2,000th trained air gunner in July. By now the nationalities under training at Morpeth included large contingents of Free French and Norwegians alongside the Poles and others. From the late summer onwards much of the training also involved the use of cine film guns which enabled performances to be assessed on the ground afterwards. This was also a benefit for nearby fighter squadrons as squadrons from both Acklington and Boulmer flew extensive fighter co-operation sorties which helped hone their skills in the run-up to D-Day.

The airfield also played host to a morale boosting tour of employees from The North East Aircraft Corporation Ltd (from Gateshead) and Northern Coachbuilders Ltd who were engaged on the construction of Fairey Swordfish and Barracuda aircraft. The tour, in September, witnessed a flying display given by a Swordfish and a Barracuda of the Fleet Air Arm.

As winter pressed in, flying training continued but at a slower pace as the runways and taxiways of the airfield were beginning to show signs of wear and tear after two years of continuous heavy training operations. As a result of this repairs were begun in December to ensure that the station could continue in its duties.

The presence of the airfield near to Morpeth resulted in a great deal of interaction between locals and service personnel. Although, as we have seen there was some friction, the overwhelming attitude was extremely supportive and Morpethians were largely proud of the airmen on their doorsteps. Indeed the popularity of the RAF was at an all-time high with many being particularly proud of the bombing offensive which was being increasingly taken to Germany throughout the year. In February, it was announced that Morpeth Urban and Rural Districts would once again come together to raise funds during a 'Wings for Victory Week' in May. The preliminary meeting held at Morpeth and chaired by the town's Mayor, Councillor J.S. Jobling, decided that the week would be between 8 and 15 May and that the initial target would be set at £140,000 (over £5,800,000 today). The area had already raised a similar sum during its Warship Week. The sum, it was believed, would enable the government to purchase an entire squadron of Bristol Beaufighters and a large depiction of the type in action was placed outside the town hall in Morpeth.

Even before the event, excitement was building and support pouring in from both businesses and locals. Lloyds, Barclays, Martins and Midland banks had all agreed to donate £5,000 apiece, while the North British and Mercantile Insurance Company had contributed £2,000 and the Northumberland Local Authorities Superannuation Joint Committee had donated £700 making a total of £22,700 by mid-April.

Part of Morpeth's success in kick-starting its fundraising efforts was in its use of street groups from selected localities in the town. This not only gave a boost through increasing community spirit but also encouraged each separate street to attempt to better its neighbours for local bragging rights. Once again street groups were asked to set their own targets and go to it. Demonstrating the duality of wealth in Morpeth the targets set ranged from £10 to £1,000 as follows (there were others which are not quoted):

Morpeth Street Groups Targets for Wings for Victory Week 1943.

Street Group	Target (£)
Auburn Place	400
Barmoor	80
De Merley	1,000
Duncan Gardens	400
Dunelm	500
Hebron	100
High School	500
Hollon Street	250
Kendor	500
Loansdean (I)	500
Loansdean (II)	1,000
Newgate Street	65
Olympia	35
Pretoria Avenue	150
St George's Hospital	60
St George's War Workers	150
St Mary's Field (I)	50
St Mary's Field (II)	25
Armstrong Terrace	15
Edward Street	10
Hood Street	15
Total	**5,805**

As the campaign opened a total indicator was erected outside the town hall so that Morpethians could follow the progress of the campaign. Programmes were also sold to raise funds, with the promise that one would entitle the lucky purchaser to a mystery prize.

A major part of the campaign was the creation of a fine display at the Corn Exchange which included models of different types of RAF aircraft, engines, dinghies, weapons, camera equipment and clothing. A number of RAF personnel were present throughout to explain the exhibits to the interested crowds who visited the exhibition. The highlight was the casing for a 500lb bomb, which visitors could leave savings stamps on in order to have the bomb filled and subsequently dropped on Germany. Throughout the build-up to the campaign and during the week itself the people of Morpeth were urged to stick their stamps on the bomb to 'help it on its way'.[129] On 12 May a large parade was held through Morpeth, which saw large crowds from the town and from the surrounding area. The parade was led by the RAF Headquarters Band and included large contingents from the RAF, WAAF, Royal Navy, Wrens, the Army, Grammar School Cadets and National Fire Service. After assembling in the Market Place the parade followed a route around Newgate Street, Howard Street, Dark Lane and Bridge Street before the salute was taken outside the town hall by the mayor and Group Captain Louden. Addressing the parade the mayor stated that 'he was delighted to have had the pleasure of thanking them for their attendance', adding that he was sure the parade would have 'been of considerable assistance to them in the middle of Wings for Victory week'.[130]

Following the parade a concert was held at the parochial hall with music supplied by the band of the RAF. The concert was a great success with large crowds attending and a significant amount of money raised for the RAF Benevolent Fund. This was followed over the next two nights later by further dances at the town hall. On the Thursday night a dance was held with music provided by 'The Morpeth Minstrels' and the RAF Band with tickets costing 1s and 2s. The following night the dance was in aid of both the benevolent fund and the mayor's fund for the mobile canteen. The smaller rural communities around Morpeth were also keen to play their part in the week-long campaign. The village of Linton had set itself the task of raising £1,000 and arranged a crowded week of events of which the highlight was a concert at the village cinema organised by the Miners' Welfare Committee. Other features included a photographic display by the RAF and a parade of youth organisations and the Home Guard.

At Lynemouth, the nursing cadets organised a similar concert featuring performances from themselves, locals and the RAF 'Spitfire Blues' Dance Band. Once again the show was a success with 6-year-old Joan Cooper's performance of *You are my Sunshine* being particularly warmly applauded. One of the organisers, Dr Skene, thanked the performers and drew attention to how the RAF men could 'laugh and joke compared to the dour, sullen attitude of their enemies'. This one concert raised over £15 for the campaign; similar events were held at Pegswood, Stobswood and Ulgham.

By the end of the week, the activities of some of the street groups could be assessed and it was found that, once again, all had greatly exceeded the target which had been set:

Morpeth Street Groups Fundraising during Wings for Victory Week 1943.

Street Group	Amount Raised (£)	Initial Target (£)
Alexandra Road	122	30
Allery Banks	37	10
Armstrong Terrace	98	15
Barmoor	315	80
De Merlay	1,774	1,000
Duncan Gardens	606	100
Dunelm	1,042	500
Edward Street	53	10
Fernleigh	773	250
Hebron	280	100
Hollon Street	1,030	250
Olympia	85	35
Stobhillgate (II)	87	45
St George's War Workers	323	150
St James' Terrace	150	20
St Mary's Field (II)	110	25
W. Greens	80	50
Loansdean (I)	828	500
Loansdean (II)	3,000	1,000
Willows	653	20
Auburn	441	400
Pretoria	465	150
Wansbeck	71	15
Total	12,423	4,755

Thus, we can see that the people of Morpeth, at least, were still eagerly supporting the war effort through fundraising efforts despite this now being the fifth year of the war. Just from this selection of street groups the initial expectations had been exceeded by over 261 per cent with Armstrong Terrace raising over 653 per cent of its intended target and the Loansdean (II) group raising £2,000 over its initial aim.

Although the urban district of Morpeth raised the majority of the funds the rural district also played a major part in the campaign raising the sum of £62,000 (almost £2,600,000 today). Once again it was the well-organised group collection areas which came in for the most praise with organisers claiming that 'great credit is due to the members of the group collections who were on their toes right from start to finish'.[131] Others to receive extensive thanks and praise were those who had made small but vital donations, local schools, the ARP services and the Home Guard, Red Cross and Fire Services who had all organised collections and events. Despite the difficulties faced by people within the rural district of Morpeth it was calculated that the contribution made by small savers in this are amounted to £3 7s 4d per person (over £125 today).

The communities of Pegswood, Broomhill, Lynemouth, Linton, Stobswood and Ellington all had extensive programmes which took place throughout the week and ensured that all of their targets were broken easily. At Pegswood the target of £4,000 was beaten and a further £87 for the purchasing of certificates under the auspices of the Aged Miners' Homes Association. The raising of this additional money (over £3,600 today) demonstrated the willingness of small local groups and organisations to get involved and is a clear indicator of not only high morale but also of a keen willingness to continue supporting the war effort and the services. In addition to this was a separate gift, inspired perhaps from the display in the town hall at Morpeth, of £26 6s 9d from the senior school for the purchase of three fighter dinghies.

Small Contributors to the Fund of the Aged Miners' Homes Association.

Group or Individual	Amount Donated
Local Tradespeople	£19 18s 4d
Mr F. Smart	£5 6s 10d
Home Guard Football Team	£7 10d
Mr E. Turner	£11 9d
Mr R. Howe	£3
Red Cross Cadets	£5 1s
Mrs R. Munday	£1 10d
Mrs T. Millar	£3 2s 6d
Master D. Hunt	16s
Mrs Mitchell	£1 4s 2d
Pegswood Colliery Welfare Committee	£29 8s 9d

From the rural district's contribution of over £60,000 it was clear that most areas had exceeded their targets. After the final tallies were counted it was found that this was indeed the case.

Sample Breakdown of Contributions in Morpeth Rural District.

Community	Target	Amount Raised
Felton	£35	£138 8s
Ellington		£1,345 16s
Stobswood	£325	£1,477
Lynemouth (small savers)		£2,068
Lynemouth (gift)		£121 6s 11d
Red Row		£2,345 18s 6d
Linton		£599 12s 8d

When the campaign ended and the sums were finally counted as a whole it was found that the target sum had been exceeded and that Morpeth and District had in fact raised the phenomenal sum of £142,240 (over £5,950,000). In the first week of June, the members of the organising committee met at Morpeth Town Hall to celebrate the success and to review the work that had been undertaken. During the course of the meeting certificates were awarded to several locals who had made significant contributions to the fundraising efforts. It was also announced that the secretary of the committee, Mr W. Raitt, MBE, had been awarded the MSE in recognition of his contribution to the National Savings movement. The mayor, Councillor James S. Jobling, also received high praise for his efforts in fundraising over the course of the previous year while Mr Malcolm Wood and Mr Hugh Swinbourne Carr were also acknowledged for their work.

Both the mayor and Mr Raitt commented that at the time of the launch of the campaign they both believed that the district had set itself a difficult, perhaps impossible, target and Mr Raitt said that he 'had expected a glorious failure' but that Morpeth and district had risen magnificently to the challenge set them with the small saver contributing 60 per cent of the funds. In an area like Morpeth, which had no significant industrial development, there were significant problems but the people of the area had demonstrated a very praiseworthy attitude towards the campaign and had acted magnificently.

Praise for the success of the campaign came in many forms with letters of congratulation from the Right Honourable, Lord Kennet (chair of the National Savings committee), and from the Chancellor of the Exchequer. In September, both Morpeth Borough Council and Morpeth Rural District Council received commemorative plaques from the RAF. The mayor of Morpeth, in accepting the plaque, stated that it would be hung in the council chamber as a reminder to all who entered of what had been achieved. Morpeth Rural District Council also presented the RAF representative (Group Captain Maskell) with two log-books to be presented to the pilots of two of the Beaufighters and expressed the best wishes of the people of the district and the hope that at the end of the war the log-books might be returned 'showing a record of success upon success'.[132]

Competition between districts in south-east Northumberland was fierce and the success of both Morpeth and Ashington during their respective 'Wings for Victory' weeks fed this attitude. Bedlington set itself the target of raising £60,000 but inspired by the example of neighbouring communities succeeded in raising £89,200. During the week there were film shows, whist drives and the inevitable dances and parades. An exhibition of model aircraft at Bedlington Station Senior School was hailed a great success as was an open day at Cambois Council School. Once again small organisations made a significant contribution with Ashington and Bedlington Civil Defence cricket teams contesting a hard-fought match at West Sleekburn and the three flights of the Bedlington Squadron of the ATS holding an aircraft quiz at their Bedlington High School headquarters.

All of this healthy competition led to Newbiggin setting the ambitious target of £45,000 in order to fund the purchase of nine Typhoon aircraft. In order to succeed, the people of the district would have to contribute on average the sum of £5 5s per head. Newbiggin was collaborating with North Seaton during the week and a packed schedule was planned. Launching the week was a parade from all the services featuring four bands and a salute. The third day was selected for a great many children's activities with sports events and a children's concert party in the Welfare Ground, while, for the sporting-minded adult, this day also saw the final of the Red Cross cricket competition. The rest of the week was dedicated to local events with dances and concerts on every night and a Newbiggin versus RAF cricket match at the Welfare Ground.

Fundraising efforts continued to be superbly supported throughout the year. When the final tally was made it was discovered that the Morpeth district Wings for Victory target of £140,000 had been exceeded with a total of £142,120 being raised. This represented an average of £5 12s 8d per head of population with small savers contributing £84,903 and large savers £57,217.

The people of south-east Northumberland were rightfully proud of the achievements of their loved ones in the armed forces but this pride also extended to those in the voluntary services. In early May, the service and dedication of two Northumbrian nurses from the Voluntary Aid Detachment (VAD) was recognised when they were awarded the British Empire Medal by the queen in a ceremony at Buckingham Palace. Nurse Susan Proudlock Tait of Morrison Road, Morpeth, and her companion, Nurse Joan Wylie of Chollerton, had been on duty at a north-east hospital when a sudden air raid resulted in a bomb demolishing the ward in which they were working. Although both were severely injured they immediately set about the work of rescuing and evacuating those in their care with Nurse Tait carrying on this work until she collapsed as a result of her injuries.

Poles became a particularly common sight in and around Morpeth as there was a considerable number of Polish servicemen based in the area, especially at RAF Morpeth. Large numbers of Polish refugees also arrived in the area and were housed locally. It quickly became clear that the increasingly large Polish community required its own medical facilities and so Frank Buddle Atkinson rented his substantial home, Gallowhill Hall, near Whalton for use as a Polish hospital. Mr Buddle Atkinson charged the Polish Paderewski Hospital, based at Edinburgh University, £600 per year to use the 51-room mansion.

The official opening ceremony in early May attracted a crowd of well-wishers including the Secretary of State in the Polish Ministry of Labour and Social Welfare, Dr Grossfeld, the Director of the Health Department of the Polish Ministry, Colonel Babecki, and the Liaison Officer to the Polish, Colonel Fortescue, and many who had offered donations to the cause. In his opening address Dr Grossfeld stated the necessity of the facility due to the suffering experienced by the Polish people exclaiming that 'Every life that could be saved had to be saved!'[133]

There was an unfortunate incident at Gallowhill Hall before the hospital had even been officially opened. A patient at the hospital, Stanislaw Sloma, had his attaché case stolen by his roommate, Stefen Toefil Sloma. The case contained £50, a camera, two watches, a platinum ring, gold bracelet, army pay book and wallet (a total value of £121 16s (over £5,000 today)). Sloma had fought in Poland, France and in the Middle East but his health had broken down and he had been discharged from the army. After this he had been sent to various Polish hospitals but had continually absconded from them. Sloma was arrested in Glasgow and confessed his guilt telling the police that he had gambled away the £50 and had sold the other items in London and other places for small sums of money. When before magistrates at Morpeth, Sloma was also charged with failing to notify the registration officer of his movements. However, Sloma appears to have been treated in a far more generous manner than many who came before the bench for similar crimes and was merely moved to Durham pending further treatment at Gallowhill Hall.

Relations with the Poles were usually friendly, although there were some tensions, and there was a great deal of sympathy expressed for the suffering that these people had experienced. Events were routinely scheduled to try to integrate and entertain the Poles. Typical of these was an event in June at a stately home where recuperating Polish servicemen were entertained by the Bedlington Collieries Band. Although language was a barrier the atmosphere was warm with each group being 'so anxious to be friendly and helpful'.[134]

The influx of servicemen into the area did lead to some problems with some of these men having criminal backgrounds and finding wartime Northumberland to be a rich source for criminality. In May, Morpeth magistrates heard what they described as 'the worst case we have had to deal with recently' when the actions of Aircraftman 1st Class Reg Gregan (22), a Newcastle man, were presented to them. AC1 Gregan had an extremely troubled past, having begun stealing from shops while employed as a teenage butcher's apprentice in Newcastle. In 1936, aged 15, Gregan had appeared before Newcastle Assizes charged with housebreaking, for which he was bound over. The next year he was again before magistrates in his home town charged this time with larceny and receiving stolen goods. The same year he was also charged, again, with housebreaking and was sent to Ponteland Homes but immediately absconded. He then appeared at West Kent, again for housebreaking, and he was sentenced to three years in a borstal. In 1940, he once again appeared before Newcastle magistrates. Charged with larceny, Gregan was found guilty and sentenced to six months' hard labour. Upon serving this sentence Gregan came out and joined the RAF. On 4 May, Gregan, based at RAF Morpeth, entered a wash room and saw a fellow patron put a wallet, in which there was money, into his coat pocket before hanging his coat up. Gregan immediately pocketed the wallet and left. He was caught by PC Grigor and charged with the theft of the wallet containing £25 in notes, 10s in coins, a Polish identity card, an RAF identity card and 2s 6d in stamps. Further investigations also saw him charged with the theft of a pair of shoes from a hut at his base. PC Grigor was able to retrieve the wallet, £23 in notes and the identity cards. The bench, aware of the criminal past of AC1 Gregan, were determined to make an example of him and sentenced him to six months for each charge and told Gregan that he was very fortunate that 'the magistrates did not decide that the sentences should not run consecutively'.[135]

South-east Northumberland had always been a popular area for vegetable shows and there was a keen sense of rivalry amongst the local leek clubs, especially in mining areas. The popularity of the 'Dig for Victory' campaign had only enhanced this despite the wartime difficulties of longer hours and obtaining seeds. As the war ground on, flower and produce shows were a means not only of providing some form of entertainment but also of boosting morale and encouraging people to grow their own food. In October, the Ponteland Vegetable and Flower Show attracted large crowds with leek and onion classes being particularly hard fought. The prizes on offer were substantial with Mr E. Frizzell of Whalton, for example, winning £2 and the silver cup for the best locally grown leek, while the open leek class prize of £20 (over £800) went to Mr James Richardson of Fawdon.

Casualties

As previously mentioned, a large number of Northumbrians had been taken prisoner during the fall of Singapore and Hong Kong. One of these men was Private Aaron Hedley Dixon of the Middlesex Regiment. A native of Morpeth, his parents lived at Blackhill and 'Aaronsfield', nothing had been heard of Private Dixon since July 1942, when it had been confirmed that he had been captured on Christmas Day 1941 during the fall of Hong Kong. In early June, a note arrived from Aaron addressed to his mother from a PoW camp. In the short note Private Dixon said that he was 'quite safe and well, and there is no need to worry about me any more'. This must have brought cheer to his parents but unfortunately it was false hope and 23-year-old Private Dixon's confidence was misplaced. Tragically, it appears that Private Dixon had in fact died in captivity some eight months previously with the note obviously having been misplaced somehow en route.[136]

The time it could take for letters from prisoners of the Japanese to reach their families led to such tragedies on more than one occasion. At the end of the year another Morpeth family suffered such a tragedy. Fusilier Gavin Dirom was another territorial in the 9th Royal Northumberland Fusiliers who had been taken prisoner at Singapore. From a farming family in the Kirknewton area, Fusilier Dirom's family had moved to a farm at High Common, Morpeth, before the war. Dirom (22) had seen active service in France and been evacuated from Dunkirk, before being sent to the east. Taken prisoner his parents received three cards from him with the last arriving on 31 December. Sadly, Fusilier Dirom had in fact died of avitaminosis, malaria and dysentery at the Chungkai Camp on the infamous Burma-Siam railway on 23 November 1943. Like many parents in such a terrible position, the Diroms simply heard no more of their only son until his death was confirmed in July 1945. In the month that his death was confirmed, Fusilier Dirom's parents placed a piece in the roll of honour column of *The Journal*. It read 'Treasured memories of our dear only son … remembered by his loving mother, father and family and all relations. Too dearly loved to be forgotten'.[137]

Another family also received news of a loved one from a Japanese PoW camp in June. These were the parents of Fusilier William (Billy) Walker of Netherton Colliery. Before the war, Billy had worked for John Douggie of Morpeth before finding employment with the United Automobile Company Ltd. A territorial in the 9th Royal Northumberland Fusiliers he had served in France before being posted to the east. The last letter his family had received had been in January 1942 when he was stationed in India but a further note in June 1943 informed them that he had been taken prisoner at Singapore and was in the Malai Camp. Thankfully, Fusilier Walker survived the experience.

We have already seen the heavy casualties which were being sustained amongst the men of Bomber Command and in 1943 the trend accelerated with the launch of Sir Arthur Harris's main offensive against the cities of Germany.

At the end of October, Mr and Mrs Richard Gray of 37 Third Row, Linton Colliery, Morpeth, received confirmation that their son William, who had been posted missing after an operation in May, was now listed as missing believed killed in action. William Dixon Gray had been a good pupil at Linton Council School and had earned himself a scholarship to attend Morpeth Grammar School where he spent five years. After leaving school William obtained work in the office at Linton Colliery but joined up shortly after the war began. Volunteering for aircrew duty William was selected for navigational training and was sent to the USA and Canada to complete the majority of his aircrew navigator training syllabus. Aged 20 in 1943 Sergeant William Dixon Gray was posted to 35 (Madras Presidency) Squadron at RAF Gravely as navigator in the crew of Sergeant A.R. Sargent. A member of 8th (Pathfinder) Group, 35 Squadron was responsible for leading bombing raids and marking targets with flares, as such they were exposed to even greater danger at times.

On the night of 29 May Sergeant Sargent's crew took off from Gravely in their Halifax II (W7876 TL-K) tasked with a raid on Wuppertal. The raid was a part of the Battle of the Ruhr and W7876 was one of 719 aircraft from Bomber Command to take part in the operation. The raid has been called 'the outstanding success of the Battle of the Ruhr' with huge amounts of damage being caused and a small firestorm developing in the town. Approximately 1,000 acres of the old centre of the town were burnt out, over 80 per cent of the town's major industrial concerns were destroyed and 211 smaller industrial premises were also destroyed. An estimated 3,400 people were killed. Losses for Bomber Command were thirty-three aircraft including ten Halifaxes of which W7876 was one. It later transpired that Sergeant Sargent's crew had been shot down in the early hours by a night-fighter. Fortunately, five of the crew managed to escape the bomber to be taken prisoner but Sergeant Gray and the crew's rear gunner, Flight Sergeant Colin Henry Garner, were killed.[138]

Although Bomber Command suffered severe casualties, its activities caught the imagination of the general public and found widespread support. The public welcomed the news that at least one part of the armed forces was taking the attack to Germany itself and few had any moral qualms after the blitz and the hardships of the previous years. Newspaper reports of raids were a constant throughout the war, especially after Bomber Harris began his main offensive in 1943. The reports always endeavoured to put a positive spin on the news of RAF raids even though, at times, they had to admit that there had been casualties. The reports were widely read and increased the support for the bombing campaign.

On 23 February *The Journal* carried a headline of '100 "Big Bombs" fell on Bremen'. The story referred to a raid launched on the night of Sunday,

21 February.[139] Although only a medium-sized raid consisting of 143 aircraft (mainly Lancasters but accompanied by 7 Stirlings and 6 Halifaxes) the report informed readers of the glow of fires being seen through thick cloud. The newspaper was also at pains to point out the industrial importance of Bremen, citing the number of aircraft and engineering plants, oil refineries and shipbuilding facilities in the city. The official report also confidently told of how over 100 of the 4,000lb bombs known to aircrew as 'cookies' had fallen on the city during the attack and triumphantly declared that no aircraft had been lost in the raid, despite heavy anti-aircraft fire over the target. Indeed, no aircraft were lost but the bombing through thick cloud meant that there were no bombing photographs to assess the success of the raid.

Alongside these accounts of bombing raids was the publication of local casualties sustained during them. Given the nature of bomber operations it sometimes took a great deal of time to provide any clarity to anxious relatives who had received a bald telegram notifying them that a loved one was missing after an operation. The Ashington family of Mr and Mrs W. Armstrong of Woodhorn Road faced a wait of several months after their 21-year-old son, Chester, was posted missing following a raid on 13/14 July. It was not until December that they received word that their son was now 'believed to have lost his life as a result of air operations'.

Flying as navigator in a Lancaster II of 115 Squadron, based at East Wretham, Pilot Officer Armstrong had taken off just after midnight for a raid on the town of Aachen. The Lancaster (DS660 KO-P) was shot down over France by a night-fighter and crashed in the Pas-de-Calais. Six of the seven-man crew of Flying Officer R.B. Larson, RCAF, were killed, with only the pilot surviving.[140]

Pilot Officer Armstrong had been educated at Bedlington Secondary School, Bede College and St John's, York and had been planning a career as a teacher before volunteering for aircrew duties.

At least one other south-east Northumberland man lost his life on this raid. Nineteen-year-old Sergeant John Foggon of Blyth was the flight engineer in a Halifax II (DT769 EQ-J) of 408 (Moose) Squadron, RCAF, based at Leeming. Shot down by the night-fighter of Leutnant Rolf Bussmann of Nachtjagdgeschwader I, five of the Halifax crew were killed. The navigator and air bomber were taken prisoners of war.[141]

It was not only the airmen of Bomber Command who became victims of the vicious aerial fighting. Another Northumbrian to lose his life on 14 July while engaged in aerial operations was Sergeant Alan Clark of Seaton Burn. Flying in a Halifax of 295 Squadron, Sergeant Clark's crew were towing a Horsa glider to North Africa when they were attacked by two Focke Wulf Fw-200 Condors. During the attack the Horsa cast off and ditched in the sea while the Halifax was shot down and six of the crew were lost. The pilot of the Halifax was the acting commanding officer of 295 Squadron, Wing Commander (acting) Arthur Bernard Wilkinson, DFC (USA).[142]

CHAPTER 6

1944: Turning the Tide

Although the government was becoming very concerned with the production of coal, the miners of south-east Northumberland continued to work exhausting hours. The miners at West Sleekburn Colliery, in particular, were singled out for praise. In February, it was announced that between June 1942 and December 1943 the workers at this colliery had never failed to reach their production targets. The final months of 1943 had been particularly trying as over 20 per cent of the workforce was off sick but those who did work put in the extra effort to match and even surpass their targets. In contrast the best month had been June 1943 when the colliery had beaten its production target by 1,399 tons. Given the shortage of qualified miners, a significant contribution was made by the more elderly miners. One flat housed seven hewers aged 55 to 64 who between them had managed to produce 50 to 60 tons every day.

Minor crime, and particularly youth crime, had been a severe problem in Blyth for some months and the occasion of the appointment of a new magistrate in the town allowed the authorities to express their disapproval over what they saw as the lack of magistrates for an area of such a large population. While the rural Coquetdale ward, with its small population, had nine magistrates and Bedlington, with 25,000 inhabitants, had fourteen, Blyth, with a population of 34,000 had only eleven. One of the problems facing Blyth was due to its importance as a port. This resulted in many cases concerned with shipping and with crewmen coming before the town magistrates. Special courts had to be held to prevent cases dragging on and resulting in ships missing their convoys and costing a great deal of money. This placed further pressure on the overstretched magistrates. A further perceived problem was in the lack of female magistrates and police officers. However, the town authorities had already petitioned to have a small number of female officers posted to the town but the request had been refused.

A meeting of the Bedlington Brewster Sessions held in February saw the police report that arrests and convictions for drunkenness were down by almost 40 per cent from 1942 with just ninety-four prosecutions. Of the cases some 68 per cent were heard at Blyth but the police were at pains to point out that 60 per cent of these involved seamen from the ships in the port.

With the Battle of Berlin fresh in the minds of the populace and the awareness of the contribution and sacrifices which airmen were making, it was no surprise that the local squadrons of the Air Training Corps (ATC) enjoyed a significant boost to their memberships. We have already seen how successful the Morpeth squadron was but at Newbiggin the squadron was still somewhat concerned over membership (possibly due to larger numbers of youngsters having a closer connection to the sea in this town) and throughout February the town hosted a recruitment campaign. The campaign sought to get Newbiggin men and women to join either the ATC, the RAF or the WAAF. Campaigners highlighted the need of the local ATC squadron and offered the allurement of training by regular RAF officers, including range firing and flights from local aerodromes.

Throughout the war there were many complaints about the perceived black-market supply of many foodstuffs, particularly meat. Butchers and hoteliers were often the target for these grumbles but at the end of February the people of Morpeth were given some proof that their suspicions were not completely without foundation. The magistrates sat for seven hours listening to a case which involved eleven charges against each of the owners of the Queen's Head Hotel and Ernest Sanderson, a butcher of Bridge Street. It was alleged that between January and May 1943 he had supplied excess quantities of meat to the hotel in contravention of the rationing system.

The case arose from allegations which had been made by the manager of the butcher's shop, Mr Lewis Carr Glendinning of Ashington. Mr Glendinning had been employed by Mr Sanderson after the latter had had an operation but the two men did not get on, with arguments over the cash register leading to Mr Glendinning being dismissed after six months. Mr Glendinning claimed that the over-supply of meat to the Queen's Head was carried out solely on the orders of Mr Sanderson. The solicitor representing Mr Sanderson attempted to make out that Mr Glendinning had been overcharging customers and that, after being caught by Mr Sanderson, had made the allegations from spite. He also claimed that Glendinning had been attempting to find out what testimony other witnesses in the case would give but this was objected to. Mr Glendinning was then accused of having attempted to overcharge at least two women and that on one occasion this led to a furious row with Mr Sanderson. Other allegations against Mr Glendinning included falsifying accounts, further occasions when he was suspected of overcharging customers and one occasion when he was alleged to have struck Mr Sanderson and chased him around the shop. After lengthy deliberation the bench returned with a verdict on one of the allegations. They were 'unanimously of opinion that the whole thing is unsatisfactory' and, as a result, fined both Mr Sanderson and the owners of the Queen's Head (Messrs McEwan) the sum of £10 apiece.

On a far smaller case Mr Norman Henderson of 408 Longwell Terrace, Pegswood, was charged with having made an untruthful declaration over the slaughter of a pig on 1 December 1943. Mr Henderson was secretary of the local pig club and kept a number of pigs himself, including one which he was being paid to look after by Mrs O'Brien, the proprietor of the Black Bull Hotel, Morpeth. Mrs O'Brien had never fed or looked after the pig but had paid for its food and when the pig was slaughtered, after Mr Henderson had applied for a licence, he had delivered the carcass to Mrs O'Brien on 15 December. Mr Henderson was told that he had committed an offence when he had signed the licence for slaughter declaring that he was sole owner of the pig and that, as secretary of a pig club, he should also have known that it was illegal to keep a pig for someone else. Mr Henderson said in testimony that he was 'trying to do the lady a good turn' with no serious intent of wrongdoing.[143]

Mrs O'Brien was instructed to plead guilty to the charge of having received meat through improper channels. In her defence it was described how Mrs O'Brien's husband had kept pigs before the war, having a sty provided by the corporation and more behind the Black Bull. He was now in the army and, after he had joined up, Mr Henderson had approached her and offered to keep a pig for her. Mrs O'Brien had agreed to pay the costs of food and had provided some swill from the hotel. She had relied upon Mr Henderson, as secretary of a pig club, to ensure that everything was above board but had been let down. In what seems to have been a rather niggardly prosecution the magistrates found both Mr Henderson and Mrs O'Brien guilty, fining Henderson £3 with £1 1s costs and Mrs O'Brien the sum of £1 with similar costs.

We have already heard of how a Mr Wilson of Cambois had rescued the driver of a horse and cart at Cambois ferry. In late February both he and the other man who had been knocked down by the runaway horse and cart attempted to claim compensation from the Co-operative Society. Both Mr Wilson and Mr Edwards claimed that they had been off work for a fortnight as a result of their injuries (both worked at local collieries) with Mr Edward also claiming £10 for the loss of his bicycle, which had been smashed during the incident. Their case was based on an obscure bye-law which stated that horses should be led onto the ferry, not driven. However, the driver, 17-year-old milk roundsman Joseph Hepworth stated that he was unaware of this as he had never taken a horse onto the ferry before and two men who worked on the ferry stated that the majority of horse-drawn vehicles were driven on. Judge Richardson, sitting at Morpeth County Court, decided that no blame was attached to the driver and that the whole matter was an unfortunate accident and found in favour of the Co-operative Society, even awarding them costs.

The blackout claimed another victim in a road accident at Ashington when a young soldier, Private Norman Aggas (20) of South Shields, crashed the vehicle he was driving into the back of an RAF lorry which had pulled over after its driver had been temporarily blinded by the headlights of an oncoming bus.

In March, the councillors of Morpeth Borough and Morpeth Rural District gathered to discuss the forthcoming Salute the Soldier campaign which was to run in the first week of June. The area had already had success with other fundraising efforts and set the ambitious target of raising enough money,

£125,000 (£5,233,000 today), to equip and clothe an infantry battalion of the Royal Northumberland Fusiliers. The honorary secretary, Mr Raitt, said that the savings effort was a continuous one and produced figures for the war years.

War Savings, Morpeth Borough and Morpeth Rural District.

Year	War Savings (£)
1940	234,000
1941	310,000
1942	337,000
1943	326,000

Mr Raitt pointed out the small drop between 1942 and 1943 and said that an analysis had shown that the small savers were contributing more but that donations from the big savers were down slightly and this had affected the Wings for Victory campaign. Despite this, the Wings for Victory campaign had still been a triumph with the target being exceeded.

A number of suggestions as to fundraising efforts were made including the involvement of the numerous armed forces detachments in the area, especially the band of the King's Own Yorkshire Light Infantry, who were stationed locally. A military parade in Morpeth, band concerts in both Morpeth and Pegswood, shop window displays and film shows were also suggested. Mr Swinburne Carr agreed to mount a display for the façade of the town hall which featured a lifted blackout and light streaming from the windows and door onto a soldier being welcomed home by his family.

Although the British Restaurants had generally speaking been a great success, a meeting of the Seaton Valley Urban Council in March heard how two such restaurants in this area were failing due to a lack of patronage. The Shiremoor British Restaurant had made a loss of £404 and the management and staff were given one month's notice to close down. Despite a petition from sixty-seven local residents for the restaurant to remain open the council agreed that it should close due to a lack of patronage. The British Restaurant at Klondyke, meanwhile, had made a small loss of £3 but it was agreed to keep the site open on a weekly basis as it was used by men employed by a local contractor.

The meeting, like many others at the time, was also concerned with post-war housing and the councillors were annoyed at the perceived interference from the regional planning officer who had objected to the siting of housing developments at Seghill and Klondyke. The council's own planning officer disagreed with the conclusions and, given that £15,500 had already been spent on roads and sewers, the council agreed to make representations to the Ministry of Health pointing out very strongly that the regional planning officer should not be allowed to impede progress.

April saw the loss of a well-known Ashington landmark. Shortly after 5 am on the morning of 4 April PC Hastie was patrolling his beat in Ashington when he noticed flames coming from the blacked out Princess Ballroom. The Princess was one of the top ballrooms in the North-East and provided facilities for dancing, musical entertainment and roller skating. PC Hastie quickly summoned the fire brigade who arrived promptly but the blaze had spread very quickly and reinforcements were summoned, resulting in units from Ashington, Bedlington, Newbiggin, Morpeth and the Durham and Northumberland Rescue and Fire Brigades attending the blaze, commanded by Divisional Officer W.S. Symons, Company Officer Outterside and Superintendent Worswick. Firemen evacuated horses and cattle from a stable on one side of the venue, while efforts also had to be made to prevent the fire from spreading to an adjoining paint shop owned by the Co-operative Society. Unfortunately, the best efforts of the firemen were in vain and the roof of the ballroom fell in shooting flames over 100ft into the sky. Within two hours the ballroom was completely burnt out.

NFS firemen damp down the wreckage of the Princess Ballroom in Ashington. (Evening Chronicle)

A gorse fire which broke out on Blyth Links had a tragic outcome on 13 April. Firemen of the NFS assisted by soldiers were attempting to extinguish the fire when there was an explosion, possibly as a result of the explosion of a mine or gas main, which killed four men and injured a number of others. The dead included three NFS firemen. Leading Fireman George William Callaway (39) was a married man who lived at 8 East Row, Blyth, Leading Fireman Richard Cecil Harris of Gladstone Street, Blyth, and Fireman Leonard Harrison (31), a married man from Sheffield who was stationed at Wallsend. Amongst the injured was Fireman John Tweedy of Queen's Road, Seaton Sluice. Fireman Tweedy was taken to hospital with serious injuries but appears to have recovered.[144]

On the same day that the three NFS men lost their lives, a Pegswood miner pleaded guilty at Northumberland Assizes to a charge of fraudulent conversion. Norman Henderson (40) had been off work following an accident and was, at the time, Pegswood secretary of the highly successful Morpeth and District Pig Club. It was alleged that in carrying out this role Mr Henderson had defrauded the club of £91 13s 10d (almost £3,900 today). The initial investigation had revealed a wider fraud in the club and another defendant, Arthur Fram (24), a miner of Sanderson's Gardens, Morpeth, and treasurer of the club, pleaded guilty to two charges involving £79 18s 6½d and £23 17s 4d (almost £4,400 today). After the first investigation the secretary of the club, Mr Appleby, had approached Mr Fram but did not obtain a suitable answer; as a result he suspended Mr Fram from his duties. It then emerged that, although suspended, Mr Fram had continued to collect money from members and had pocketed this himself (this was the second charge of £23). Mr Fram was sentenced to six months' hard labour and Mr Henderson received a fine of £10. Judge Richardson stated that there had been laxity in the running of the club and that it was foolish to have set up the club without taking legal advice. In defence of the club it had started in a very small way but had proven very successful and had expanded quickly as a result.

At the start of May there was a tragic case brought before the bench at Blyth. It was alleged that Herbert Albert Balls (22), a labourer and driver from Seaton Sluice, had attempted to poison his estranged wife, Mrs Margaret Balls (18). Mrs Balls described how she had left her husband after six months because he would not work and had attempted to force her to borrow money from a money lender. She had received a letter from her husband (she was living with her parents in Blyth) asking her to meet him in Ridley Park, Blyth, to discuss their marital problems. On the appointed day Mrs Balls took her young baby to the park and met with her husband. The two sat in a shelter and talked about their problems, with Mr Balls entreating her to return to him. When she refused, he became excited and produced a small bottle which he claimed contained enough poison to kill the three of them and showed her a note he had written describing why he had committed suicide. The two then struggled with Mr Balls dropping some of the liquid onto the ground and a few drops onto his wife's face, resulting in burns. Mrs Burns screamed for help and the green attendant, James Blyth, subdued Mr Balls and secured the bottle. Mr Balls asked Mr Blyth to throw away the bottle but he refused and it was later passed onto the police.

After being questioned by the police, Mr Balls said that he was not serious in his attempt but merely intended to scare his wife into returning. He did not deny what had happened but said that his mind was disturbed as he had been extremely distressed after his wife left him. An analysis of the liquid revealed that it was 'killed spirits of salts' used in soldering and although it was very corrosive the amount in the bottle was unlikely to have caused death.[145] Mr Balls' case was set aside for the next assizes meeting.

Although the invasion of France seemed to now be growing nearer, the men of the Home Guard continued in their duties of defending Britain. May gave many of the local units the chance to celebrate the fourth anniversary of the formation of the force. In Morpeth a large parade and service was held on Sunday, 7 May. The parade, inspected by Colonel Hawkins, took place on Grange House Field and there was a very large turnout. Officers on parade included: the commanding officer Lieutenant Colonel G.L. Rutherford; the second-in-command Major J.A. Flint; Captain Stenhouse, adjutant; Major G.F. Howell; Major Swanston; Major Catcheside; Major Pumphrey; and Major G. Fail. Music was provided by the band of the DLI and the Reverend J.M. Lloyd conducted the service.

On Saturday, 13 May, the 17th Battalion Northumberland Home Guard held an anniversary dinner at Ashington. The Loyal Toast was proposed by Lieutenant Colonel Cruddas with Captain W. Gibson proposing a toast to the guests who were present. Answering this toast Lieutenant Colonel H. Skinner-Brown, sub-district medical officer of Stakeford recollected that four years previously the Home Guard 'were armed not to the teeth but with not much more than their teeth'. On this day, however, the Home Guard was now well equipped for anything which lay ahead of them but it was important that, despite the optimistic war news, they realise that the fighting was not over and the battle not yet won. Lieutenant Colonel Cruddas praised the spirit and determination of the men for never showing any trace of defeatism even when equipment was short. Organised by administration officer Captain G.S. Slim, the evening was capped off by musical entertainment provided by a number of performers including: Normanton Barron and his Orchestra; well-known Morpeth baritone Stan Pearson; boy accordionist A.J. Armstrong; vocalist J. Ross; and Lieutenant J. Brownrigg, a humorous singer. Other entertainers included impersonators E. Richardson and J. Taylor. A large number of officers attended the dinner, as listed here. Zone, sector and sub-district officers: Colonel Viscount Allendale; Colonel A.E. Hawkins; Colonel F. Straker; Lieutenant Colonel

H. Skinner-Brown; Major P. Sellars; and Major H. Lawson. Principal officers of the 17th Battalion: Lieutenant Colonel B. Cruddas; Major W.N. Craigs; Major W. MacFarlane; Major J. Abercrombie; Major A.S.E. Richards; Major W.G. Robinson; Major N. Carmichael; Captain H. Powner; Captain G.S. Slim; and Captain A.B.H. Irvine. Guests from neighbouring battalions: Colonel G. Rutherford; Lieutenant Colonel A. Laird; Major G. Catcheside; Major J.A. Flint; and Captain H. Cookerham.

At Ulgham, the Home Guard held a dance to celebrate the anniversary and to raise funds for the Red Cross. Held at the parish hall the event saw a number of competitions and was a great success, raising the sum of £5 14s 9d for the Red Cross.

Voluntarism and enthusiasm for the military services continued unabated throughout 1944, especially amongst the young. Regular Sunday parades were very well attended, providing continuing support for 404 (Morpeth) Squadron of the Air Training Corps. On Saturday, 27 May, the squadron, along with others of the area, was inspected by Air Marshal Sir Leslie Gossage, the Chief Commandant of the ATC. Many graduates of the squadron went on to join the RAF and the training they had received proved to be of great value to them. One such example was that of Aircraftman 2nd Class G.A. Bates. In his preliminary examination for air crew training he gained a score of 100 per cent in mathematics and averaged over 87 per cent in English, modern history, geography and science.

Bedlington-born Lieutenant John Butcher, fought in France, Tunisia and Italy. (Evening Chronicle)

While the newspapers were full of accounts of D-Day the *Evening Chronicle* still managed to carry an account of a Bedlington man who was fighting in Italy. Lieutenant John Butcher had worked at the Doctor Pit before the war but joined up and fought with the Grenadier Guards in France before being wounded during the escape from Dunkirk. After his recovery he was commissioned and retrained as a tank commander before being posted to Tunisia. Once the Germans had been driven out Lieutenant Butcher took part in the fighting in Italy. The newspaper reported how he was the commander of the reconnaissance tanks of the 8th Army which made the important link-up with the US 5th Army shortly before the entry into Rome. Sadly, Lieutenant Butcher was killed just one day after his story had appeared in the newspaper.[146]

Although the successful D-Day landings were greeted with relief and celebration there were numerous south-east Northumberland families who suffered the loss of a loved one on that fateful day. The men who crewed the various landing craft on D-Day had an immensely important and dangerous task. One such young man was Petty Officer (Motor Mechanic) Robert Swinney Elliott Stafford (23). Petty Officer Stafford was a Blyth man who had worked as a farm carter before the war and on D-Day was the engineer aboard Landing Craft Tank 859, tasked with landing units from 7th Field Regiment, Royal Artillery. These consisted of eight M7 Priest Self-Propelled Guns and sixteen towed 25-pdr anti-tank guns. After landing on Sword Beach the crew supervised the successful unloading of the landing craft; but as it was reversing off the beach the craft struck a mine. Petty Officer Stafford received dreadful wounds to his lower body and died several minutes later. For his actions on D-Day Petty Officer Stafford was mentioned in despatches.[147]

The men of the Royal Engineers also had vital tasks on D-Day with the clearing of obstacles, mines, securing bridges and setting up fortifications. Sapper Harold Pratt (20), 19th Field Company, Royal Engineers, the youngest son of Mr John Forster Pratt and Mrs Kate Annie Ella Pratt of 94, Ninth Row, Ashington, was killed on D-Day and subsequently buried at Bayeux War Cemetery. Sapper William Grant (22), 295th Army Field Company, Royal Engineers, was the son of Peter and Margaret Grant of Whitley Bay. Like Sapper Pratt he was killed on D-Day and is also buried at Bayeux.

On 9 June, Mr Balls, accused of attempting to poison his estranged wife, was brought before Northumberland Assizes at Newcastle. Mr Balls pleaded guilty to attempting to administer poison with the intent to endanger life and, after the court heard how Mr Balls was of previous good character, Mrs Balls gave evidence. Mr Justice Cassels appears to have taken the part of Mr Balls in his questioning of Mrs Balls and seems to have not been very impressed with Mrs Balls. Mrs Balls said that she would not return to her husband as she had their baby to think about and when Mr Justice Cassels asked her to confirm that she was not of a forgiving nature she said that that was indeed the case, before adding that her husband had badly used her and that she did not care what was done to him. The judge then said 'You are making it very difficult. Can't you find it in your heart to say anything in his favour?' Mrs Balls replied that she had experienced an unhappy marriage to which the judge asked if she was not willing to try again in her marriage to which, unsurprisingly, Mrs Balls said, 'Not again'.[148] After dismissing Mrs Balls the court heard from the Blyth probation officer that he would endeavour to bring the parties back together. Mr Justice Cassels then accepted Mr Balls' plea and bound him over and placed him on probation for two years.

Voluntarism was not, of course, solely responsible for the Home Guard as the National Service Act of 1942 had allowed compulsory conscription into the Home Guard and many 17-year-olds received their initial training in the force. By the summer of 1944 there were quite large numbers of compulsory service guardsmen of all ages and not all were, by this late stage of the war when invasion or raiding was extremely unlikely, entirely enthusiastic in attending to their Home Guard duties.[149] In September, two Tritlington brothers found themselves before Morpeth magistrates charged with having missed Home Guard parades. James Lonsdale Dowson (24) of and Roy Dowson (26), farmworkers, of Hall Farm Cottages, Tritlington, were both charged with having failed to attend three parades at Tritlington on 4, 11 and 19 July, without reasonable excuse. Inspector Stanwix gave evidence that Roy Dowson had told him that he had sent in a letter saying that the nature of his work made attendance impossible and added that two years previously he had fallen from the second storey of the town hall and injured himself, resulting in hospitalisation for some time. Inspector Stanwix had informed Roy Dowson that if that was the case then he should have submitted himself for medical examination by the Home Guard doctor. Roy's younger brother also said that he could not attend because of the nature of his work. The inspector admitted that two other Dowson brothers had been excused duty for the harvest but added evidence that the two accused were persistent offenders with Roy Dowson having attended only three parades from a possible 153 and his brother only 33.

After hearing further evidence from the Home Guard authorities, the bench found the defendants guilty and fined each brother the sum of £6 with an additional 3s 9d costs, which was payable within a fortnight or each would face a prison term of one month. The presiding magistrate explained that the decision had been reached because of the seriousness of the matter and informed the two brothers that the ruling did not exempt them from further service. He also advised them that if their farm work truly made it impossible for them to attend then they should get their employer to make a formal approach to the authorities. He concluded by telling the men that if they appeared again on similar charges they would not be fined but would be sent to prison.

The reason for some men resenting their duties in the Home Guard was largely the result of the change in the fortunes of the Allies and the resultant, and correct, view that invasion or raiding was highly unlikely. However, the majority of members realised that the Home Guard fulfilled other functions. It helped train young men before call-up to the regular army, it provided a social outlet for many men, it still helped to free regular troops up from onerous duties such as guard duty, it helped man the anti-aircraft defences of the country, and, crucially, the force had become a very useful tool for supporting local causes and communities.

Typical of the events organised, which fulfilled both a social function and raised significant funds for a worthy cause, was the supper and musical evening held in mid-August at the Drill Hall in Morpeth. The supper was held to thank the ladies of the WVS and the men of the civil defence services who had helped out at a recent Home Guards' sports meeting held on Whit Monday. The sports meeting had raised the sum of £235 for the Royal Northumberland Fusiliers Prisoners of War Fund. Speaking at the end of the evening Lieutenant Colonel Rutherford took the opportunity to thank Captain Stonehouse, the adjutant, who was stepping down to take up another military appointment.

In August, the Chief Constable of Northumberland, J. Simpson, launched a week-long 'Safety First' campaign to reduce the growing trend of road traffic accidents. Although the blackout had been a huge contributory factor, accidents in daylight had also been increasing. As part of the campaign an exhibition was opened in the town hall but the people of Morpeth were more heavily influenced (and amused) by another part of the campaign. A police officer was stationed in a building overlooking the Market Square and, equipped with a microphone, admonished poor behaviour on the road outside. One officer was no respecter of position as was shown on 16 August when one of the 'victims' was a Morpeth alderman. The unfortunate gentleman was crossing the street when the voice announced, 'Sir, I advise you not to have a conversation in the middle of the road: you might be killed.' Pedestrians and drivers were all admonished by the candid advice of the voice from above. After announcing that over 500 people were killed on the roads every month the same officer addressed a woman who was crossing, 'You, madam with the basket, have you got eyes in the back of your head? You are walking in the middle of the road without looking behind. You are indulging in jay-walking madam.'[150]

Most members of the Home Guard, therefore, remained enthusiastic. This was shown by the attendance of over 160 officers and men of the 17th Battalion who went to a weekend camp held at Ashington at the start of September. The main feature of the weekend was a marksmanship competition in various firearms. The camp was not all work, however, with Saturday night seeing a 'Go-as-you-please' variety concert, at which the most hilarious contributions were made by Sergeant Downie, Corporals Mead and Mordue, Lance Corporal Drinkwater, Private Heard, Tomlin, Baxter, and Bullough.

September also saw a rash of vegetable and flower shows across the area and the Home Guard was often involved in this pastime. When an appeal for help went out from the Young Women's Christian Association hostel on Newgate Street the members of the 3rd Northumberland (Morpeth) Battalion rose to the occasion and used their vegetable show at the Drill Hall on Copper Chare to raise funds. The show took place over the weekend of 16-17 September and attracted a large number of entrants and visitors. The women of the local WVS assisted in running the show and contributions were generous given the popularity of the hostel and its work to help women in the area. On the Sunday evening the prizes were given out by the wife of

Lieutenant Colonel Rutherford, commander of the battalion. There had been, unsurprisingly, keen competition in the leek show. The eventual winner of the Three Pot Leeks class was B. Clavering, second place went to J. Thompson of Mitford while Mr Clavering also won third place. The jam and pickle section also saw keen competition and offered a chance for the wives and mothers of Home Guards to show their skills. These classes, along with other classes of preserves, were judged by a member of the Food Advisory Bureau of the Ministry of Food. The 1lb jar of jam class was won by Mrs Roland Elliott of The Chimes Lodge, Morpeth, second place went to Mrs Flint of Morpeth, and third to Mrs Kirwan of Morpeth. The pickles class was won by Mrs G. West of Morpeth, second place was Mrs Bell and third was Sergeant McMorn. To the surprise of many, a free gift sale was also held on the Sunday.

The 'Dig for Victory' campaign had enthused many in the area with a number of newly formed allotment committees and other groups (pig clubs were especially popular). For example, the Barrington branch of the Bedlingtonshire Allotments Association held their second annual show in the Railway Inn at Choppington on 9 September. There was a very large entry to the show and after the show a large amount of the produce was sold to raise funds for the Red Cross, War Agricultural Fund and the local comforts fund. The weekend also saw a highly successful flower and vegetable show at the Victory Hall in the village of Whalton. There were twenty-seven classes in the show and, once again, the proceeds of the sale following the show went to the Red Cross and St John's Fund.

Minor crime continued to be a problem throughout the year and in the summer the theft of bicycles became a particular problem. At the same hearing as that which had sentenced the Dowson brothers, magistrates heard how Richard William Sennett (17) of 149 Bothal Terrace, Pegswood, had been arrested by PC McDonald and had confessed to having stolen a bicycle, valued at £6, from William Bell Slater of Morpeth. Mr Sennett had a previously clean record and said that he had not intended to steal the bike when he took it but was fined the sum of £2. The next case was that of Pegswood miner, Ernest Cave (40), who was charged with having unlawfully received a bicycle from Mr Sennett, who lived near him at Pegswood. It was explained how, after Sennett had stolen the bicycle, he had met with Mr Cave and his son on Whorral Bank where Mr Cave had bought the bike for £2 as he wanted it for his son.

Upon being questioned by the police Mr Cave said that he had believed Sennett's account that he had bought bike from a friend of his called Liddle for a packet of Woodbines. He had been trying to get his son a job in Morpeth and knew that he would need a bicycle to go to and from work but after working on the bike realised that he had got a bargain. Some time afterwards Mr Slater had approached him and told him that the bike was in fact his property. Mr Cave had believed him and told the bench that he had not been suspicious of the willingness of Sennett to sell the bike so cheaply. The magistrates did not believe Mr Cave, who had no previous convictions, and told him that they believed he must have suspected that the bike was stolen and that he was 'the worst offender in this case'.[151] The bench then pronounced Mr Cave guilty and fined him £2.

Other crimes were of a more serious nature and often resulted in harsh penalties as a result of stricter laws governing the production and sale of goods seen as vital to the war effort. William Allen, a miner who lived at 11 Poplar Street, Ashington, found himself charged with three offences under the Essential Works Order of 1943. It was alleged that while working underground at North Seaton, Mr Allen had failed to carry out instructions on 9, 10 and 12 November 1943. The charges related to Mr Allen having refused to couple together tubs and do similar work with the result that he had stopped work and had in turn stopped others from working. After being charged at the time of the offences the accused had said that he was not paid for work of that sort but the hearing was adjourned for six months to allow Mr Allen to do the work and prove himself. In this time he had carried out his work regularly but had been absent without excuse on two occasions. The case was dismissed after the accused agreed to pay costs and to do such work in the future.

As the fighting continued in Europe more south-east Northumbrian families received the dreadful news that a loved one had been killed. Amongst those killed who were well-known at Morpeth Grammar School was Captain Lionel Clifford Beckerleg, RASC, who was killed in action on 1 November and is buried at Bergen-Op-Zoom Canadian War Cemetery. Captain Beckerleg had been educated at Dunheved College in Launceston and London University before obtaining a master's post at Morpeth Grammar School in 1931. He was remembered as a very good teacher who also took a keen interest in cricket and football and was a married man who left behind a widow (Doreen, née Johnston) and two young children at his home at School Close, Morpeth. Captain Beckerleg was originally from St Ives where his late father had been a former mayor of the town and his family had already felt the tragedy of war when Captain Beckerleg's eldest brother had been killed during the First World War.[152]

It was announced that the Home Guard would be officially stood down on 3 December and plans began immediately to prepare parades and various other celebrations in the area. In Morpeth, the 3rd Battalion was to parade through the town and the salute would be taken at New Market by Colonel Bernard Cruddas, DSO (of Middleton Hall), the first commanding officer of the battalion, and was to be followed by a drum-head service.

The week before the parade, the officers and men of 'B' Company, Battle Platoon, 17th Northumberland (Ashington) Home Guard, held their own stand-down supper. The platoon, commanded by Lieutenant J. Ferguson, had won the field firing competition at the sub-district contest and the trophy and individual awards were handed out at the supper. 'B' Company commander, Major A.S.E. Richards, was also awarded with a cake dish by Lieutenant H. Allison on behalf of the officers and men of the company. Major Richards said in his speech that although the Home Guard was being stood down he thought it 'a sin that such a collection of men should be allowed to scatter to the far winds without being of use to themselves or the nation'. He suggested that the Home Guard could be of great use to the Army Cadet Corps and urged the comradeship of the Home Guard to be retained through the creation of rifle clubs or, at the very least, an annual reunion.

Colonel A.E. Hawkins of 2nd Northumberland (Alnwick) Battalion marvelled at the proficiency which had been attained by the men of the Northumberland Home Guard and stated that it was the existence of a large and well-trained and equipped Home Guard which had allowed such a vast British Army force to embark upon the D-Day landings. Colonel Cruddas also praised the men before handing out the awards. The award winners were: Lieutenant J. Ferguson; Sergeants J. Downie, R. Walkinshaw, J. Wilshaw; Corporals J. Smith, H. Charlton, A. Russell, T.O. Doherty, J. Chapman, L. Hewitson, and R. Reed; Lance Corporals J.G. Wren, W. Wren, and G. Wilson; Privates J. Johnson, T. Nesbit, R. Gardener, T.S. Ditchburn, J. Ditchburn, A. Nesbit, R. Savage, F. Talbot, F. Marsh, and J. Gray.

On the night before the stand-down parade, the officers and men of 'A' Company of the 3rd Battalion held their own stand-down supper at the Drill Hall. The supper was very well attended with everyone very enthusiastic to celebrate the Home Guard. One speaker stated that he was 'sure that our days in Britain's vast unpaid army will ever be remembered with pleasure and satisfaction'. The company commander, Major G.F. Howell, was joined at the head table by Colonel Cruddas, Lieutenant Colonel Rutherford, Major Flint and other officers along with the guest of honour, the mayor. After proposing the toast to the king, Major Howell reminded the men that they were being stood down, not disbanded, and that, in a crisis, they might be recalled.

Major Flint, who had been involved in the initial recruitment of the company, gave the toast to 'A' Company. He explained how in the early days there had been a slow, but steady, stream of recruits following the initial wave of recruitment on 25 May 1940. He also explained some of the difficulties they had faced with many of the men of the town already serving in the ARP or civil defence services. He gave particular praise to the many veterans who had formed the core of the company and particularly praised those who had stayed in service throughout (while admitting that some had not stayed the course). He also praised the young men who had come forward admitting that without them 'the mobility of the company would have been of a low degree'.[153] Major Flint went on to praise the men for their consistent high standards, stating that the fact they had been able to parade as a company (whereas other members of 3rd Btn had not) had been a great help in achieving this efficiency.

Responding to Major Flint's praise and toast, Major Howell thanked him and praised him for his early endeavours in raising the company when it was ill-equipped and 'expected to face the whole German Army with rifles from the Grammar School, and one clip of ammunition'. He acknowledged that many enjoyed looking back on the early days of the LDV with fondness for the purely volunteer nature of the force when everyone had '100 per cent enthusiasm'. This, he claimed was the true spirit of democracy but he believed that this enthusiasm was still present and had not been diluted or affected by conscription into the force. He also signalled one note of dissatisfaction when he said that he had been disappointed by the references in the press to the German Home Guard telling his comrades that there was 'a whole world of difference between our Home Guard and those hordes of miserable slaves hounded into the trenches by the German Gestapo'.[154]

There followed toasts to the guests, especially to Colonel Cruddas, who was praised for his early efforts, Lieutenant Colonel Rutherford and the mayor. In his address, Colonel Rutherford firstly thanked the ladies who had prepared the supper and admitted that this was the fifth battalion dinner he had attended. He praised the comradeship of the men and urged them to do their best to maintain it even after stand-down but admitted that he regretted the fact the entire battalion could not be assembled in its entirety more often than it had. He also took the opportunity to push the idea of aiding the British Legion in constructing a hall in Morpeth. Colonel Cruddas thanked the men for their invitation to the stand-down parade and expressed his disappointment at the earlier decision to split the original 3rd Battalion into two (at which point he had left) due to the size of the area it had to cover. The mayor, who had been an original member of the company when it had formed, also praised the men for their comradeship and spirit of self-sacrifice.

Lieutenant E. Fail, commander of the Morpeth Battle Platoon, was awarded an inscribed silver tankard from the NCOs and men in his charge. The Morpeth Battle Platoon had won three of the four competitions which the battalion had held (platoon drill, battle drill, and the night patrol) and had tied for the fourth (platoon in attack) with the Netherton Battle Platoon. Unfortunately, from his perspective the Netherton Platoon had been selected for the sub-district competition and had been narrowly beaten by the Ashington Platoon. Major Howell concluded by expressing his gratitude to Mr Johnstone of Grange House Farm for allowing the company the use of his fields for range practice. The evening was brought to a close with musical entertainment.

Unfortunately, when the day of the stand-down parade arrived, rain caused a change in the plan with the service at Morpeth being moved inside to the Coliseum. The parade was, however, very well attended with many of the men looking upon it as a farewell occasion. Following the parade through the town the officers and men went into the Coliseum where the service was taken by the

Reverend W. Goode. He was joined on the stage by Colonel Cruddas, Lieutenant Colonel Rutherford (the commanding officer), Colonel Glendinning, Major Flint, Captain E.W. Weeks, Captain Ridley, Captain Sims and the Mayor, Councillor J.S. Jobling, in full regalia. Music was provided by the Seaton Colliery Band.

After the opening hymns, the Reverend Goode addressed the officers and men saying that it was an honour to be taking the service. Unfortunately, his opening address could best be described as rambling as he praised the men for their activities praising the quality of discipline but rather oddly extolling this virtue with the example of Singapore. In his opening address he stated:

> *They had done their duty, and now receive the thanks of the country for what they had done. Those leaving the Home Guard, could take something away with them. He was sure they could. They came under discipline and what a wonderful thing discipline was. Without it the Army was lost. Singapore lived for ever as a [sic] example of discipline; learned to do what they were told. It had been a good thing for this country.*[155]

After extolling discipline at some length, the reverend went on to praise comradeship, instructing the men to take these qualities with them into their private lives. He then went on to praise the self-sacrifice of the men of the Home Guard before again urging the men to take this quality with them as they left its service, urging them to ensure that they did not rest until they had done their bit to make the world a better place for coming generations.

After this speech, Colonel Cruddas thanked the officers and men of the battalion for giving him the honour of addressing them and reading the king's message to them. The king's message was rather more fulsome in its praise of the activities of the Home Guard and the service then concluded with another hymn and the singing of the National Anthem.

Dinners and suppers celebrating the Home Guard continued throughout the month with the officers and men of 'A' Company, 17th Northumberland (Ashington) Home Guard enjoying their stand-down supper on 16 December at the Ashington Drill Hall. The supper presented the officers and men with the chance to thank their commanding officer, Major J. Abercrombie, MBE, MM, who had led them with enthusiasm and vigour for four years. Lieutenant Colonel Straker in his speech recalled his twenty years' service in the Northumberland Hussars and how Major Abercrombie, who had then been a Sergeant Major, had taught him a great deal even though he was of senior rank. Given the leadership abilities of Major Abercrombie he was sure that 'A' Company had benefitted greatly. He completed his address by saying that he hoped that the spirit of co-operation which had been a key feature of the Home Guard would be continued by the men after the stand-down.

There followed some humorous anecdotes about Major Abercrombie from Lieutenant J.E. Parkinson and then expressions of gratitude from Colonel

Cruddas, Colonel Hawkins (the sub-district commander) and the Ashington Urban District Council. The toast of the night was to Major Abercrombie and was delivered by his second-in-command, Captain H.P. Wilson, who said that the major had enjoyed good health during the past four years and added, humorously, that the company had 'suffered his good health'. As to the suggestion that a history of the 17th Battalion should be written he said that if it took eight volumes then seven of them would be about the major. Praising his leadership qualities, he concluded that Major Abercrombie had 'all the qualities of a good soldier and the character of a good Northumbrian'.[156] The toast was supported by Sergeant R. Miles and the whole company joined in giving a roaring chorus of 'Old Soldiers never Die'. Following a brief speech by the Company Sergeant Major, George Lynch, a cake stand was presented to the major by Captain Wilson.

A toast was then given to the guests by Lieutenant G. Fleming and was responded to by several of the guests including Councillor F. Millican, a trade union leader, who introduced a political note into his speech when he said that he knew the miners would have hoped to have been able to stand with their countrymen on foreign battlefields but had been told they were in a vital industry and had, therefore, remained at their jobs and had gladly volunteered their free time to the Home Guard. He then remarked that he was pleased to hear such expressions of hope for 'sincere post-war co-operation'. Another guest, Major J.C.R. Cookson, added that from his prior military experience he knew that the miners made very good fighting men.

Shortly after this supper the men of the 'C' Company at Newbiggin held their own supper at which the commanding officer, Major J. Downie, and his wife were given a biscuit bowl which the major accepted on behalf of the company which, he said, had been a privilege to command. He also expressed the thanks that were owed to the previous company commander, Mr Robinson, and his wife for their role in the early days of the war. At Lynemouth, the officers and men bade a farewell to 'D' Company commander, Major N. Carmichael, MM, while, at Linton, Lieutenant J. Miller took charge of the proceedings

Although most people were in the last stages of their Christmas preparations, the desire to raise funds for the Red Cross continued to find favour. On the day before Christmas Eve, a pigeon, rabbit and poultry show was held at Morpeth Town Hall. As it was a Saturday it was thought the event would be well attended but, probably because of the closeness to Christmas, there were not as many entries as expected, although the standard was high. Competitors came from as far away as Durham with a Mr Harrison of that city winning the pigeon section. The rabbit section was won by someone closer to home: Mr T. Thompson of Pegswood. Because of the season and the weather conditions the final section (that of poultry) was combined so that the entrants could get home safely.

CHAPTER 7

1945: Victory & Peace

The New Year opened with the announcement that a Blyth minister had demonstrated 'outstanding courage on the battlefield' during an action in the Ardennes. The Reverend Whitfield Foy (28) was attached to the 6th Airborne Division and had parachuted into France on D-Day. During a heavy mortar barrage he had volunteered to lead a search party to locate and rescue some wounded British soldiers. The brave Methodist minister (of Wensleydale Terrace) and his party managed to successfully rescue several soldiers. Reverend Foy was the son of a miner and had been educated at Blyth Secondary School before becoming assistant minister on a Leeds circuit. He had married a woman from his hometown (she was a teacher at Newsham) and his brother, Gilbert Foy, served on Blyth Town Council.

As the fighting continued in Europe the people of the area continued their support for the various charitable causes which had proven so popular during the war. The information officer of the British Red Cross and Order of St John of Jerusalem wrote from his office at 39 Newgate Street in Morpeth to express his thanks for the continued donations to the Prisoners-of-War Parcel Fund throughout February. Donations came from a very wide variety of sources including private donations and community collection boxes from across south-east Northumberland.

Donor (collection boxes)	Amount
Mrs Smith, 32 Fourth Row, Ashington	£2 8s 9d
Mrs E. Cowling, Hood St, Morpeth	5s
Mrs Dirom, High Common Farm, Morpeth	£1 1s 3d
Mrs Oldfield, 15 Strong's Buildings, Scotland Gate	5s
Mrs Walker, 4 South Front Row, Choppington Colliery	5s
St.George's Hospital War Workers, Morpeth	£2 1s 6d
Miss Simpson, 14 Howard Road, Morpeth	£4
Mrs Humphrey, 8 Vernon Place, Newbiggin	£2 2s 4d
Donor (private)	**Amount**
Messrs R & I Hewitt Ltd, Pottery Banks, Morpeth	14s 1d
Ellington Youth Club	£1 2s
Mrs R.C. Oliver, Bowmer Bank, Morpeth	£5 5s
Ministry of Supply, Hartford	£1 6s 10d

Others were also keen to continue making a contribution and when a dance held by Morpeth Police Recreation Club at the Town Hall on 21 February made a profit of £29 10d it was agreed to disburse the funds to five different charities. They were: Morpeth Welcome Home Fund (£15); the local branch of the Red Cross (£5 10d); Morpeth Dispensary (£3); Poor Children's Holiday Association (£3); and Northumberland Nursing Association (£3).

Despite the momentous events that were taking place, many people continued to enjoy what hobbies they could. The Wansbeck Angling Association held its annual meeting at the Queen's Head Hotel, Morpeth, in the first week of March. Bolstered by the large numbers of resident servicemen who had joined the association during the war the chair was able to inform the well-attended meeting (the majority coming from Morpeth, Pegswood and Ashington) that the association had a credit balance of £115 18s 1d (almost £5,000 today). The board asked the members to agree to the raising of annual fees as the service personnel who had led to the increased profits would, presumably, be leaving the area shortly. Although this might be unpopular, members were urged to vote in favour because the price of stocking the river had increased dramatically (1,000 trout now cost £22) and were reassured that the healthy financial position of the association meant that it was in a good position to bid for further fishing rights as and when they came available. As a result, the members were convinced, although there was one vote against, and the prices (which had not risen in 38 years) were raised so that a 1946 season permit would cost 7s 6d for established members, 12s 6d for new members and remained at 2s 6d for the young and old members.

By the first week of May, it was increasingly clear that Germany's surrender would be announced any day and people began eagerly planning celebrations. In Ashington, flags and bunting were put out on the day before the announcement was made (this was due to a German broadcast which came before the official British announcement) and people were noticeably more cheerful on the streets of the town. 'Wansbeck', the correspondent who wrote the regular 'An Ashington Widow' column in the *Morpeth Herald*, hinted, however, at some of the resentments which had built up in the town during the war. In the column dated 11 May she wrote that with the early news of peace restraint was understandably lacking and that the celebrations could be excused but also that it was forgivable and understandable to 'even hurl bricks at the windows of shopkeepers who, for the duration of the war, have coldly ignored our pitiful pleadings for a share of that little bit of something extra which has for so many years resided coyly beneath the counter'. Continuing the criticism of shopkeepers the writer described how many had quickly taken advantage of the demand for red, white and blue flags and bunting and how some had quickly sold out despite the fact that 'to put out flags to celebrate the peace was quite an expensive business'.[157] Others were less concerned over such matters with one Ashington schoolboy, after being released from lessons on VE Day, asking if the news meant that they might, at last, get some bananas.

Even with victory over Germany being so close, the people of Ashington remained firmly committed to the men of the ship which the town had adopted. When the sports officer of HMS *Blackpool* wrote asking for help in the purchase of football equipment for the crew, the sum of £30 9*s* was quickly raised (£1,250 today). After the equipment and postage had been paid there was still £9 4*s* 8*d* left, which was sent to the crew with orders to spend it on whatever they needed (almost £380).[158]

The courts, however, carried on business as usual with a variety of cases being heard across south-east Northumberland in the days before VE Day. On the day before the announcement of victory a soldier found himself before the bench at Bedlington charged with having stolen items worth £42. Stanley Ginnever (25) was based at Hartford Bridge Camp but was alleged to have broken into a house named 'Highfield' in Bedlington and stolen a handbag containing three ration books, three registration identity cards, three clothing ration books, £5 15*s* in cash, a gold cigarette case, a gold matchbox case and four gold sovereigns. All were the property of Mary Georgina and Albert Chisholm. The crime was said to have taken place on 15 March. By mid-April, the police had recovered the gold cigarette case and matchbox holder, which had seemingly been sold on in Newcastle. At the end of the month Detective Constable Scott and Inspector Durman visited the accused and, in the presence of his officer, told him of their suspicions. After initially denying all knowledge of the theft, Ginnever was taken to Bedlington police station where he asked to make a statement. In this he confessed to the crime saying that on the night in question he had visited friends and had been walking home when he noticed the big house. He had walked up the driveway, entered the premises through a partially open window and stolen the bag and its contents. After selling the items (now recovered) he had hidden the bag. Charged with the theft Ginnever stated that he was sorry and 'would not have done it if I had known it would have caused all this inconvenience'.[159]

The weather on VE Day morning was quite good but the afternoon and evening were rainy. The people of Morpeth, however, quickly took to the streets to celebrate Germany's surrender with the town being bedecked with flags and bunting. Street parties, dances and bonfires were well attended with people eager to celebrate, even those who had lost loved ones. A dance had been organised in the town hall and the tickets quickly sold out but those who had been left disappointed assembled outside in the Market Place and danced outside. The dance, organised on behalf of the mayor and mayoress by Mr P.R. Soulsby, was a great success with the music of Percy Hall's Dance Band being very welcome. The dance itself raised £45 (almost £1,850 today) for the Welcome Home Fund.

VE Day teas were a common sight across south-east Northumberland despite the poor weather on the day. At Sheepwash, a large tea was held on Sheepwash Bank with musical accompaniment provided by locals playing violin and accordion, as well as the inevitable gramophone. Likewise, the Newbiggin streets were bedecked with flags and bunting with street parties, followed by races, dancing and music. In Pegswood there were also street parties but some, after attending the VE Day Thanksgiving Service at Morpeth Road Methodist Church, chose instead to go to the concert which had been organised by the Pegswood Wesley Guild on behalf of the Welcome Home Fund. These scenes were repeated across the area including at Ashington where there were street parties, and an open-air dance, held at the People's Park, attracted a large crowd, despite the inclement weather. The local authority plans for a huge bonfire were frustrated 'by the cautious enforcement of the dim-out regulations in the coastal belt'. Such pernickety enforcement, however, meant little to most of the ordinary folk of the town and a large number of unofficial bonfires were lit with numerous effigies of Hitler being cast into the flames. Streets were decorated and many of the brick air raid shelters had 'V' signs painted on them in red, white and blue. Pianos, radios, gramophones and tables and chairs were dragged into streets and the parties were quickly organised with the energy 'for which the inhabitants of the colliery rows have a special talent'.[160]

VE Day was not only about celebration, however, there were also a large number of thanksgiving services held across the area. At St James' in Morpeth a solemn and impressive service was well attended. While giving thanks for victory and offering prayers for the people of Europe who had suffered (and in many cases continued to do so) prayers and remembrance were also offered for the many people of Morpeth who had been killed, injured, had spent time in captivity or had suffered loss of loved ones. The Reverend G.W. Lane warned that 'I think there is a danger that we, as a people, are likely to forget the history of the past six years. It is essential that we should remember these years.'[161]

The following day was also declared a public holiday and the weather this time co-operated, resulting in a number of VE Day teas taking place across the town. In Praetoria Avenue, Morpeth, garage proprietor, Mr O. Elliott, prepared a VE Day tea party. Two long trestle tables were decorated with flags and bunting and, by the afternoon were laden with cakes and confectionery. After the local children had enjoyed the food they were taken onto the boats and given a trip along the river before going to the cinema. West Greens celebrated with a similar street party. Organised by Mrs Rogerson and Mrs Brattle, the neighbourhood combined to ensure that approximately 120 children enjoyed a feast of homemade scones, buns, sandwiches and cakes while the street was colourfully decorated. After the tea a variety of sports and games had been arranged with locals aged between 4 and 60 taking part. Prizes were awarded for some events with Mrs Stansfield winning a table runner, which had been offered by Mrs Rogerson, and Mrs R. Payne winning a half-dozen eggs which had been offered by Mrs Brattle. After the sports, a game of musical chairs took place followed by dancing accompanied by Mr T. Rogerson on the piano accordion. At Eastview Square, Middle Greens, a Union Jack used in the celebration was the same one that had been used in a similar event in 1918. Once again, children (this time from Edward Street, Allery Banks and Eastview) enjoyed a tea followed by sports and games. The children of Edward Street seem to have had a choice of venue as a tea was also held for them, and the children of Castle Street. Once again, both streets were decorated and teabread and cakes served before a programme of dancing and singing. Music was supplied by the gramophone of Mr Ralph Payne. After darkness had fallen here an effigy of Hitler was burnt in the lane, much to the amusement of the children. Mr Soulsby, again, and a Mr Charles Fagan organised an outdoor evening dance and entertainment in New Market. Music was supplied by Mr Bliss and consisted of the broadcasting of dance music from 6 pm until 9 pm. The dance was very well attended with both adults and children enjoying the festivities. Members of the forces who were present in Morpeth were certainly not left out, with the committee of the YMCA in the Market Place supplying free refreshment and entertainment to 3,000 service personnel while their colleagues in the YMCA at the parochial hall also supplied free refreshments. The good weather on the day following VE Day resulted in even more street parties in Ashington, while almost 2,000 people of the town attended a public thanksgiving service which was held in the greyhound stadium.

Morpeth airman Charles Fairbairn was, by the end of the war in Europe, a Warrant Officer and had been flying Liberators with RAF Coastal Command. Having already been invested with the DFM in 1944 for his actions during his first operational tour with Bomber Command, Warrant Officer Fairbairn would have particularly enjoyed attending Buckingham Palace on the day following VE Day when he was invested with the Distinguished Service Medal (DSM) by the king. Warrant Officer Fairbairn, of 30 Hollon Street, Morpeth, was not the only Northumbrian RAF Warrant Officer to be so awarded on that day as he was accompanied by Warrant Officer Robert Robson of Weetslade Crescent, Dudley. Two other men from south-east Northumberland were awarded the British Empire Medal at this investiture. They were Second Lieutenant Walter Bell, York & Lancaster Regiment, from Morpeth, and Mr Alan Burt, Able Seaman in the Merchant Navy, from Gladstone Street in Blyth.

RAF Acklington had been largely inactive throughout much of the latter part of the previous year while reconstruction work had been undertaken. Barring the brief stay of a unit of Vought Corsairs of the RN this inactivity continued until 59 OTU was reformed at Acklington at the end of February. Training fighter-bomber pilots the unit was equipped with the Typhoon Ib as its main equipment. With the end of the war in Europe there was a substantial scaling back of recruitment and training of RAF flight crew. As a result of this only one course graduated from the unit before it was disbanded on 6 June. This was not the end of Acklington as an active station, however. In May, the commanding officer, Wing Commander G.W. Petre, of the airfield welcomed the North American Mustang IV fighters of 19 Squadron.[162] The squadron flew a variety of training missions during its time at Acklington and there were two losses during the period. On 12 June, Flight Lieutenant Young was killed when he crashed into the sea after descending through cloud, and just over a week later Flight Lieutenant Robson was killed when he crashed into high ground near Berwick in foggy conditions.[163] The squadron left in August and for the remainder of the war Acklington was home to the night-fighter Mosquito NF.XXXs of 219 Squadron.

On 15 May (just one week after VE Day) the axe fell on 57 OTU at RAF Eshott. Students who were sufficiently advanced in their training were transferred to the few OTUs which were still operating. Three days afterwards, 289 Squadron flew into Eshott after being transferred from nearby RAF Acklington. The squadron was a mixed one equipped with the Spitfire XVI and the rare Vultee Vengeance IV. This somewhat cumbersome-appearing aircraft was the only specifically designed dive bomber to operate in a close support role with the RAF but had been replaced by the Mosquito. In keeping with its role as an anti-aircraft squadron 289's Vengeances had been modified to serve as target tugs. Days later, 289 Squadron was joined at Eshott by another target tug squadron when 291 Squadron arrived from Yorkshire. It too was equipped with the Vengeance but added to the assortment of aircraft at Eshott with its Miles Martinet Is and Hurricane IIs. The two squadrons did not remain long at Eshott with both having departed at the start of June to be disbanded.[164]

A little under a month later, on the anniversary of D-Day, 57 OTU was officially disbanded and RAF Eshott's satellite field at Boulmer was closed down. The aircraft used by the unit were flown out, with some going to the remaining training units but the majority being transferred to RAF maintenance units to await scrapping. This marked the end of Eshott as an operational airfield although from October it was used as a satellite site by 261 Maintenance Unit which was based at RAF Morpeth.[165]

At RAF Morpeth 4 AGS had been disbanded at the start of December 1944 with the airfield being unused for some time. At the end of April, however, 80 (French) OTU was formed at Morpeth. The unit was formed to train French pilots to fly the Spitfire (four French Spitfire squadrons were based in Germany with the 2nd Tactical Air Force). The OTU was equipped with four aircraft types: ex-service Spitfire IXs were joined by several Miles Master IIs, Miles Martinet Is, and a lone DH Dominie II. Once again, the stay of this unit was short and in July, 80 (French) OTU moved the short distance west to RAF Ouston, ending the wartime flying career of RAF Morpeth. In September, however, 261 MU was transferred to Morpeth.[166]

A Vultee Vengeance dive bomber (this one in service with 12 RAAF Squadron). (PD)

RAF Ouston had played home to 62 OTU since 1943 and the unit continued to grow as the war in Europe approached its conclusion.[167] In March, 62 OTU, already a large unit, was enlarged once more as almost 30 Vickers Wellington XVIIs and XVIIIs were allocated to the unit for radar training.[168] At the same time 23 Hawker Hurricanes arrived to be utilised as moving targets for the trainee radar operators. Despite the overcrowding on the airfield, accident rates were kept low although just days before VE Day the unit sustained its only Hurricane loss, when LF644 became victim to an engine failure.[169] Less than a month later the OTU was disbanded. As mentioned above, the next unit to arrive was 80 (French) OTU with its Spitfires.[170]

The Morpeth iron foundry and works of Swinney Bros Ltd was widely praised both for the contribution it made to the war effort in terms of production (the firm was widely involved in the making of ship fittings and shell cases) and for the willingness of its employees to enter service in the forces. Over the course of the war some seventy men employed by the firm served, with two of them being killed. These were Sergeant C. Christie and Able Seaman N. Martin. There was an intriguing story in the local press after the war, regarding two men, J.N. Broad and W. Young, who were killed while employed in the drawing office. It seems that the two men had accompanied a warship out to sea on its sea trials but on the first afternoon out the vessel was attacked and sunk (I can find little further evidence of these men).[171] Shortly after the war, a dinner was held to celebrate the work of the firm and its contribution to the economy of the town. At this dinner several awards were handed out for long service with Mr Alexander Dippie receiving particular praise for his sixty-three years' continuous service to the firm. During his service Mr Dippie had lost an eye (in 1887) and a hand. As a result of the latter injury he was placed in charge of the gate house. During the war he was instructed not to let anyone not employed by the firm enter the works unless they had a pass and so seriously did he take his duties that when a highly placed official from the Admiralty arrived he was told that he would have to report to the office in Dacre Street like anyone else![172]

A tragic death occurred just five days before the end of the war when Company Sergeant Major Frederick George Johnson (29), Yorks and Lancs Regiment, was killed when the army lorry in which he was a passenger crashed on Bothal Bank. The driver told the subsequent coroner's inquest that he was unfamiliar with the route and that he was still using the restricted wartime lighting despite now being allowed greater lighting. The bank at Bothal is steep and there was a tight bend to the right. He stated that he did not see the bend until it was far too late but denied having consumed any alcohol while he had been in Ashington before leaving, claiming that he had only partaken of cakes and tea. The officer who was accompanying the driver said that he was also unaware of any lifting of lighting restrictions but argued that the accident could have been avoided if the fence had been painted. Superintendent T.S. Scott stated that, because the area was heavily wooded they had asked Ashington Council to consider the painting of the fence. A verdict of accidental death was recorded.

Following the dropping of the atomic bombs on 6 and 9 August it became clear that Japan was about to surrender and many in south-east Northumberland were in celebratory mood. The residents of Hollymount, Bedlington, enjoyed a VJ Day tea on 15 August in the Locke Hall. The children who attended were presented with prayer books by the Reverend Carr of Benwell and enjoyed a bonfire and firework display in the evening. These scenes were seen across the area as bonfires were lit and communities came together to organise victory teas for children. The celebrations, however, were rather more restrained than had been expected with the years of war having proven exhausting. The very short supply of beer also curtailed some of the wilder excesses and the damp weather in the evening brought an early end to some celebrations.

Supplies, however, were still in short supply and many community groups had already used supplies and funds for the VE Day celebrations. Thus, some celebrations were delayed until after the VJ Day announcement on 15 August with victory celebrations taking place sporadically throughout the month. On 19 August, for example, the residents of Sanderson Gardens, Morpeth, had a tea and sports meeting at the hut on Proctor's Field. Each child was presented with 3*d* on behalf of the mayor and that evening the residents were joined at a dance by men from the nearby army camp. On 22 August, the residents of Stobhill Gate held their celebrations. A sports morning was organised followed by a dance in the evening.

On the following day, the residents of St Mary's Field, Morpeth, also held their victory tea and sports day at Proctor's Field (loaned by Councillor R. Dowie). The sports were held in the morning and, following this the seventy or more children sat down at tables decorated with flowers before enjoying the sausage rolls, sandwiches and cakes which had been provided. When the children had finished, the tables were replenished and the adults sat down to their own victory tea. After this a number of games and raffles were held while the group was entertained by the singing of Myrna Rutter. On leaving, once again each child was presented with 3*d* from the mayor. This was not the end of the festivities for the residents of St Mary's Field as a social and dance was held in the evening for the residents and several members of the forces, with the evening culminating in the singing of the National Anthem.

Although the families of Stobhill Gate had already held some of their celebrations with a sports event and dance they followed this up on 25 August with victory teas which were held at Second, Fifth, Sixth, and Seventh Avenues with 108 children and 20 senior citizens enjoying tea, sports and another dance.

At North Seaton, the VJ Day celebrations were quickly followed by the annual Holidays at Home festivities. Prominent amongst the many events was a pony and working horse gymkhana with over £200 in prize money being awarded for the various events. The show was very popular and those who attended also enjoyed the music provided by the North Seaton Workmen's Prize Band. One of the most popular classes was that of the pit ponies, all of which were given a rousing welcome.

Four women from Morpeth (Mrs Armstrong, Mrs Brunning, Mrs Elliott and Mrs Hedley) organised a victory tea for the children and elderly residents of Staithes Lane, Wellwood Gardens, Gas House Lane and Corporation Yard for 30 August. There were seventy children in the party with each being presented with 3*d* from the mayor. Following the tea, a fancy-dress competition was held with prizes awarded in two age classes. The winners in the first class were Billy Stanners and Thomas Robson (1st), John Gibson and Etta Stanners (2nd), Lilian Paton (3rd), and Thomas Heslop (4th). In the second class, Michael Elliott (1st), Edna Anderson (2nd), Yvonne Gosling (3rd), and Moira Owens (4th).

The end of the war also brought news of the closure of yet another local military establishment when it was announced that HMS *Elfin*, the submarine base at Blyth (which had been in operation since the First World War), was to close in September. During the war, the base had served in training 10,000 submariners and 900 officers as well as being the home base for the 6th Submarine Flotilla. Once the 1,400 officers and men had left, the plan was for the Wellesley Nautical School to resume occupation of a greatly expanded establishment.

With the end of the war many societies and organisations were keen to show what they had contributed to the war effort. At the end of August, a short piece appeared in the *Morpeth Herald* praising the efforts of the Women's Section of the British Legion, Morpeth. All the ladies were the wives, mothers and sisters of servicemen and women, former servicemen and women of the war just ended or any previous war. The article praised the way the ladies had gone about their work in a quiet manner despite losing their rooms and headquarters to the army twice at the start of the war. In 1940, the section had furnished a ward of the Emergency Hospital at Stannington and members visited the patients throughout the war. Other members served in service canteens, while those who were housebound knitted comforts for the services. Members also took part in a scheme whereby they befriended servicemen who had no family and sent comforts to them. As well as these efforts, the ladies of the section also served in civil defence services and in the WVS and nursing services. Their work continued in the early weeks of peacetime with a group accompanying 120 mothers and children to Seaton Sluice.[173]

It was not only groups such as the above that sought to publicise their wartime efforts; national and local companies were also anxious to prove their wartime bona-fides in order to curry good favour and secure peacetime trade. Throughout August there were adverts in the local press from companies such as Dunlop. This company highlighted the contributions that had been made by the company in a series of adverts, such as the development and production of nearly a million rubber-tyred wheels for tanks and other tracked vehicles.

For the many farmers in south-east Northumberland the end of the war brought new opportunities but also trepidation. With the anticipated end, or relaxation, of wartime price controls and other measures they faced a freer but more uncertain market. However, such was the world food crisis that the Ministry of Agriculture immediately poured cold water on the belief of some in the farming community that there might be an early return to peacetime conditions. At the end of August, notices appeared in the local press informing farmers that potatoes and beet crops would have to be maintained at wartime (1945) levels for at least a further year and that this acreage would be maintained through regulation if necessary. Average prices of these crops, however, would be maintained. For many arable farmers there was worse news as the wheat supply worldwide was better and this meant that although there would be no cropping directions for wheat or rye, farmers were strongly urged to sow all suitable land with wheat and rye in the national interest. Furthermore, the prices of these crops were to be halved in value from £4 to £2 per acre.

Dunlop Advert pt.2. (Morpeth Herald)

The end of the war also meant that some items which previously had been widely used by the farming community were now made available again. Many chemical supplements and items such as sheep dips were not widely available during the war as many of the chemical factories had been turned over to wartime production. The Hertfordshire firm of Cooper, McDougall & Robertson Ltd quickly placed adverts for its Border Paste Dip into the local press in south-east Northumberland. This derris-based dip, obviously targeted at a northern audience, provided weatherproofing to fleeces and protection against sheep keds and had been unavailable during the war.[174]

EVERY FARM A BETTER FARM

THE NATION NEEDS—

The very difficult world food situation has grown worse, instead of better as was hoped. It will not, therefore, be possible to allow so much freedom of cropping as was at one time expected. This applies particularly to potatoes and sugar beet.

● It is **essential** that the 1945 acreages of **potatoes** and **sugar beet** should be maintained next year. **If necessary, this will have to be done by the service and enforcement of directions.**

● There will be no reduction in the overall average prices of these two crops or in the acreage payment for potatoes.

● With **wheat,** world production is better than with most foodstuffs, but transport from producing to consuming areas still presents serious difficulties. As these difficulties are expected to lessen, no cropping directions will be served for the growing of wheat.

● As previously announced, there will accordingly be a reduction in the acreage payment from £4 to £2 per acre. **Rye** will be treated on the same lines. Nevertheless, in the national interest farmers are asked to **sow all suitable land to wheat and rye** this autumn, and not concentrate unduly on spring-sown crops in view of labour difficulties.

The Government will do everything possible to secure the necessary labour for the 1946 harvest.

Issued by The Ministry of Agriculture and Fisheries

Ministry of Agriculture and Fish Directions to Farmers, August 1945. (Morpeth Herald)

With the war over, the south-east of Northumberland could reflect on its contributions and on its future. The massive output of the area's coalfield had proven of critical importance to the war effort while the farmers of the area had made their contribution to maintaining the food supply of the country. While industry was light and widely dispersed several factories also made worthwhile contributions and the port of Blyth played a significant role in both the local shipbuilding industry (especially for lighter vessels) and in the vital East Coast maritime trade. For the future? Most councils were already well advanced in plans to replenish housing stocks but these would be badly disrupted by the lack of materials and men which were available in the immediate pre-war years. For a prosperous future there would have to be considerable development.

Endnotes

1   [T]yne & [W]ear [A]rchives [S]ervice: MB/WB/27/1 (T135/45). Whitley Bay Urban District Council (ARP Committee).

2   *Ibid.*

3   [N]ational [A]rchives: HO 187/1775. Auxiliary Fire Service: mobilisation, 1939.

4   NA: HO 187/33. Auxiliary Fire Service: conditions of service, disciplinary control, machinery for representation etc. 1936-1941.

5   NA: HO 187/50. Auxiliary Fire Service: war organisation. 1939-1942.

6   The crew were: 22-year-old Flying Officer Michael Franklin Briden (Pilot); 21-year-old Pilot Officer William Stanley Francis Brown (2nd Pilot); Sergeant Valentine Henry Garner Richardson (Observer); 19-year-old AC2 Isaac Davidson Leighton (Air Gunner); AC1 Peter John Warren (Wireless Op/Air Gunner); and AC1 Alan Gordon Foster (Wireless Op/Air Gunner). The body of AC1 Foster was later washed ashore while the others are commemorated on the Runnymede Memorial.

7   Aircraftman Leighton had been in the RAF for two years and was approaching his twentieth birthday when he lost his life. His father, Robert, and step-mother Florence lived in Dudley, Northumberland.

8   *Morpeth Herald*, 22 December 1939, p. 2.

9   *Morpeth Herald*, 22 December 1939, p. 6.

10 *Morpeth Herald*, 22 December 1939, p. 7.

11 *Morpeth Herald*, 19 January 1940, p. 1.

12 TWAS: MB/WB/27/1 (T135/45). Whitley Bay Urban District Council (ARP Committee). Notes on the exercise of 28 May 1940.

13 TWAS: MB/WB/27/1 (T135/45). Northumberland County Council booklet: ARP, 1940.

14 TWAS: MB/WB/27/1 (T135/45). Whitley Bay Urban District Council (ARP Committee).

15 *Ibid*.

16 TWAS: MB/WB/27/1 (T135/45). Whitley Bay Urban District Council (ARP Committee), report of 28 August 1940.

17 The all RAF crew were: 29-year-old Sergeant Reginald Stephen Callinan from Auckland City, New Zealand (Pilot); 26-year-old Sergeant John Samuel Scarfe (Observer); 22-year-old Leading Aircraftman Peter Murray (Air Gunner); and 20-year-old Leading Aircraftman Thomas Liddle (Air Gunner). Oddly another Northumberland man was killed in

similar circumstances almost seven months later, to the day, flying with the same squadron in an aircraft of the same type with a very similar serial number.

18 *Evening Chronicle*, 15 May 1940, p. 6.

19 *Morpeth Herald*, 31 May 1940, p. 5.

20 Foot, William, *Beaches, Fields, Streets, and Hills. The Anti-Invasion Landscapes of England, 1940* (English Heritage, 2006), p. 199.

21 *Morpeth Herald*, 28 June 1940, p. 1.

22 The property seems to have had a distinct Italian connection as the *Kelly's Directory* of 1938 lists the premises as belonging to Mr Louis Bertorelli, a confectioner.

23 *Morpeth Herald*, 3 May 1940, p. 8.

24 *Morpeth Herald*, 22 November 1940, p. 4.

25 *Evening Chronicle*, 2 March 1940, p. 5. Interestingly Clousden Hill had been the location of a short-lived social experiment, the Clousden Hill Free Communist and Cooperative Colony. This was the first anarcho-communist farming community to be set up in Britain. See: Todd, N, 'Roses and Revolutionists' (Five Leaves, 2015), and http://www.ic.org/wiki/clousden-hill/

26 *Newcastle Weekly Chronicle*, 16 November 1940, p. 5.

27 *Morpeth Herald*, 29 March 1940, p. 5.

28 *Morpeth Herald*, 12 July 1940, p. 3.

29 The deputation must have been astounded to be present at Westminster on the day after the debate on Chamberlain's (and his government's) conduct of the war had concluded and when Westminster was in a febrile turmoil as Chamberlain manoeuvred, in vain, trying to find a way to remain as PM. As they awoke in their hotel the next morning it was to the news that Germany had invaded Belgium, Luxembourg and Holland and that the Phoney War was over; by the time they reached home Winston Churchill was PM.

30 *Morpeth Herald*, 14 June 1940, p. 5.

31 *Morpeth Herald*, 17 May 1940, p. 2.

32 *Morpeth Herald*, 14 June 1940, p. 5.

33 *Morpeth Herald,* 17 May 1940, p. 2

34 *Morpeth Herald*, 17 May 1940, p. 2.

35 *Morpeth Herald*, 12 July 1940, p. 3.

36 Sergeant Atchison is buried in the Reichswald War Cemetery where his parents had 'His Memory is Our Greatest Treasure' inscribed upon his grave. The others to lose their lives were: Flying Officer T.H. Parrot (Pilot); Leading Aircraftman T. Poad (Wireless Operator/Air Gunner); and Aircraftman 2nd Class T. Jones (Wireless Operator/Air Gunner). The surviving airman was Flying Officer D. Blew (2nd Pilot) who became a prisoner of war.

37   *Evening Chronicle*, 19 September 1940, p. 5.
38   Thomas, who was from Guildford, had already led a distinguished career in the military and was to end his career in 1948 as an honorary Major General and had been Inspector General of the British Army in Burma and General Officer Commanding the British Army in Burma. He had served in the First World War with the East Surrey Regiment and had been awarded the MC in 1917 for leading a raid on German lines. After serving, and being wounded, in Iraq, he was given a permanent commission in the Northumberland Fusiliers and also served attachments to the King's African Rifles (KAR) and the Sudan Defence Force (SDF). During the Second World War he served in France, Malaya and Burma campaigns and after leaving the Northumberland Fusiliers in 1942 commanded the 1st Wiltshire Regiment and subsequently 88th and 36th Indian Infantry Brigades. At the end of the war he was awarded a CBE and a bar to his DSO; Major General Lechmere Cay Thomas, CB, CBE, DSO (and bar), MC died in 1981.
39   Captain Ernest Benjamin Lomas Hart, 9th Northumberland Fusiliers, was killed on or around 24 May 1940 during the retreat to Dunkirk aged 39. The son of Colonel E.J. Hart, OBE, of Pewsey, Wiltshire, he has no known grave and is commemorated on the Dunkirk Memorial.
40   The sinking of the Cunard liner remains the greatest maritime disaster in British history. Estimates of the dead range from 3,000 to 5,800 with 1,738 having been positively identified. Even though a neighbouring liner had been hit hours earlier and a destroyer advised the captain of the *Lancastria* to leave port and set sail he did not do so as he feared submarine attack while unescorted. Shortly before 4.00 pm three bombs hit the ship causing her to turn over and sink within 20 minutes. The resultant death toll accounted for approximately 1/3 of all BEF casualties. The news of the disaster was hushed up and only revealed two weeks after the sinking.
41   The other crew members were: Flight Lieutenant Charles David Weaver Price (pilot); Pilot Officer James Tayne Taine Fleming (navigator), a New Zealander serving in the RAF; and Sergeant Lawrence Land (wireless operator).
42   Sadly, Douglas Leonard Bisgood's luck did not hold out and he was killed, as a Squadron Leader, in a flying accident in April 1947 while acting as an RAF instructor.
43   Bungay, S, *The Most Dangerous Enemy. A History of the Battle of Britain* (Aurum, 2001), p. 214.
44   AVM Saul did not receive the recognition of his more southerly based counterparts but was in many ways an admirable man. Serving as an observer with 16 Squadron flying BE2s and RE8 reconnaissance

aircraft, by the end of 1917 he was commanding 4 Squadron (again RE8s) before undertaking a wide range of command roles in the interwar RAF. Commanding 13 Group in 1940 he not only provided protection to the north of England and Scotland but was also responsible for ensuring that the pilots which he dispatched southwards to 11 group were adequately trained and experienced. This was in stark comparison to his 12 Group counterpart AVM Leigh-Mallory. During the first days of September (the height of the Battle of Britain) the pilots sent south by Saul claimed forty-three enemy aircraft for the loss of just two pilots while those sent by Leigh-Mallory claimed just seventeen victories and lost thirteen pilots. After Leigh-Mallory took over at 11 Group, Saul found himself appointed Air Officer Commanding 12 Group and then in 1943 he took over as AOC Air Defences Eastern Mediterranean. After retiring in 1944, Saul became chairman of the United Nations Relief and Rehabilitation Administration's efforts in the Balkans before managing the university book shop at the University of Toronto. Retiring in 1959 he died in 1965, aged 74, after being struck by a car.

45   *Berwickshire News & General Advertiser*, 15 May 1945, p. 4.

46   The all RAF crew consisted of: Flight Lieutenant Louis Percy Rowley (Pilot); 25-year-old Pilot Officer Robert Archibald Hanks (Observer); 18-year-old Sergeant John Walter Purt (Wireless Op/Air Gunner); and 27-year-old Sergeant John Jackson Wilks (Wireless Op/Air Gunner). Flight Lieutenant Rowley was a very experienced pilot who had joined the RAF in 1928 as a Pilot Officer and was transferred to the reserve in 1933 as a Flying Officer but was again promoted in 1936 and seems to have been possibly serving as a civilian instructor. Horst Carganico was killed in a crash on 27 May 1944 at which time he was a Hauptmann commanding I/JG5 in the defence of Germany and was credited with sixty victories (fifty-four of which were achieved on the Eastern Front); the Hudson of Flight Lieutenant Rowley was his fourth victory. He was the son of Luftwaffe General Viktor Carganico.

47   *Yorkshire Evening Post*, 23 September 1940, p. 3. Leading Aircraftman Gordon was aged 23 at the time of his death and is buried at Seaton Valley (Cramlington) New Cemetery.

48   *Morpeth Herald*, 22 November 1940, p. 4.

49   *Morpeth Herald*, 29 November 1940, p. 1.

50   *Morpeth Herald*, 29 November 1940, p. 1.

51   TWAS: MB/WB/27/1 (T135/45). Whitley Bay Urban District Council (ARP Committee). Report on the raid of 8 December 1941.

52   Fusilier Russell is buried at Malbork Commonwealth War Cemetery.

53   [T]yne & [W]ear [A]rchives [S]ervice: MB/WB/27/1 (T135/45). Whitley Bay Urban District Council (ARP Committee), p 26.

54 *Morpeth Herald*, 28 March 1941, p. 3.

55 *Morpeth Herald*, 16 May 1941, p. 6.

56 The German crew: Oberleutnant H. Voigtlnder-Tetzner; Leutnant zur See R. Dietze; Obergefreiter W. Wesseres; and Obergefreiter H. Vandanne were all killed (Oberleutnant Voigtlnder-Tetzner's body was washed ashore and is buried at Thornaby on Tees).

57 The fire, which was centred on oil tanks and wood yards in the North Shields area, was so severe that fire crews from across the region, including Northumberland, were called in to give aid.

58 Thirty-five people were killed during the raid including, in addition to the two first aid workers, a soldier and two policemen. A further nine policemen and eighteen civil defence workers were injured, seven of them seriously.

59 Some sources refer to two casualties at Blyth but I have only been able to identify one and further research seems to show that this 'additional' casualty was in fact Mr Norfolk at Bebside.

60 Brigadier General Pawle's daughter Rosemary married Group Captain Peter Townsend, RAF, just three months after this following a whirlwind two-week courtship while Townsend was recovering from wounds.

61 *Morpeth Herald*, 25 April 1941, p. 5.

62 *Morpeth Herald*, 8 August 1941, p. 4.

63 This was, incidentally, the night when a bomb hit Wilkinson's Shelter in North Shields killing 105 people out of the 190 who were sheltering there.

64 At least one source claims that three aircraft were destroyed in the attack.

65 *Morpeth Herald*, 16 May 1941, p. 6.

66 *Morpeth Herald*, 4 September 1941, p. 2.

67 *Ibid.*

68 *Ibid.*

69 *Morpeth Herald*, 8 August 1941, p. 4.

70 *Morpeth Herald*, 8 August 1941, p. 4.

71 *Morpeth Herald*, 8 August 1941, p. 4.

72 *Morpeth Herald*, 8 August 1941, p. 4.

73 *Newcastle Evening Chronicle*, 3 October 1941, p. 4.

74 *Evening Chronicle*, 3 October 1941, p. 4.

75 The Westland Whirlwind was a heavy, fast and well-armed aircraft boasting four nose-mounted 20mm cannon and was used on strikes against rail targets before being withdrawn from service in 1943.

76 The crew were: Flying Officer Tate, DFC, (pilot); Sgt Claude William Robinson; Sgt Percy Shane; and Sgt Basil Ransome Edis. All are commemorated on the Runnymede Memorial.

77   *Daily Mirror*, 4 October 1941, p. 6.

78   Bill Stephens also played for Hartlepool Utd and Luton Town in wartime fixtures and he scored nine goals in just six appearances for Hartlepool. After the war Bill Stephens returned to Leeds Utd and in his final season at the club in 1945-6 played eleven times and scored once before being transferred to Third Division Swindon Town where he scored 27 goals in 49 matches. He subsequently played for West Ham Utd but suffered two broken legs in successive seasons and, despite scoring seven goals for the Hammers, he left for Cardiff City in 1950 but never played for the club and was forced to retire a year later. He died in 1974. Alf Stephens also played in wartime fixtures for Leeds Utd, York City and Aldershot and after the war returned to Leeds but when his brother left for Swindon Town so did Alf. The two played together for Swindon before Alf retired in 1948. He died in 1993. They remain the only twins to have scored in the same game in the Football League (21 September 1946 at home to Exeter City in a 2-0 win).

79   Happily, it appears that Sergeant Weallens did survive the war.

80   During the war the men of the RNLI rescued 6,376 people and 19 RNLI lifeboats took part in the Dunkirk evacuation.

81   *Morpeth Herald*, 19 December 1941, p. 2.

82   This day is still known to many in Hong Kong as Black Christmas.

83   Henry was a native of Stakeford while Private Smith was from Cambois and Private Logan from Hazelrigg.

84   Forty-six survivors from the SS *Shuntien* were picked up by the corvette HMS *Salvia* and between eleven and nineteen by the destroyer HMS *Heythrop*. Tragically HMS *Salvia* was torpedoed and sunk in the early hours of the next day with no survivors.

85   HMS *Blackpool* was built by Harland & Wolff at Belfast and launched in July 1940. The Bangor-Class minesweeper was formally commissioned on 3 February 1941 and served throughout the war before being sold to Norway and renamed the *Tarna*. The vessel was stricken off in 1961. The Bangor-Class vessels were derided as having poor handling qualities and being overcrowded with almost 100 crew being crammed into a vessel originally designed to hold just 40.

86   *Morpeth Herald*, 19 June 1942, p. 6.

87   *Morpeth Herald*, 17 April 1942, p. 6.

88   See Wilt, Alan F., *Food for War. Agriculture and Rearmament in Britain before the Second World War* (OUP, 2001), p. 188.

89   Despite the fact that horses were still used in the majority of labour the numbers had declined by 72,000 in the five years 1939-44.

90   *Morpeth Herald*, 24 April 1942, p. 5.

91   *Ibid.*

92   *Ibid.*
93   *Morpeth Herald*, 20 February 1942, p. 4.
94   *Morpeth Herald*, 20 February 1942, p. 4.
95   *Morpeth Herald*, 17 April 1942, p. 6.
96   *Morpeth Herald*, 3 July 1942, p. 5.
97   The 'River' class ships were: HMS *Ballinderry*; HMS *Dart*; HMS *Frome*; HMS *Ribble*; and HMS *Torridge*. The 'Castle' class included (I have not been able to find the others): HMS *Knaresborough Castle*; HMS *Launceston Castle*; and HMS *Hever Castle*. The company also built at least two 'Flower' class corvettes: HMS *Anemone*; and HMS *Arbutus* (sunk by a U-136 on 5 February 1942).
98   *Northern Daily Mail*, 4 August 1942, p. 8.
99   *Northern Daily Mail*, 6 August 1942, p. 8.
100 *Northern Daily Mail*, 18 August 1942, p. 8.
101 *Evening Chronicle*, 20 August 1942, p. 4.
102 *Sunderland Echo & Shipping Gazette*, 27 August 1942, p. 7.
103 *Daily Mirror*, 27 August 1942, p. 4.
104 *Ibid.*
105 *Sunderland Echo & Shipping Gazette*, 27 August 1942, p. 7.
106 *Morpeth Herald*, 14 August 1942, p. 3.
107 *Morpeth Herald*, 13 November 1942, p. 1.
108 Of this crew there were two more men of British nationality: Chief Cook Charles Popley (49); and Saloonman Walter Morgan (50). The U-Boat which sunk the SS *San Blas* was itself sunk by US aircraft just a fortnight later; there were no survivors.
109 *Morpeth Herald*, 19 June 1942, p. 6.
110 Like many such films the title of this last film inspired many an American airman to name his aircraft in honour of it and there were several 'Sleepytime Gals' which flew in various theatres of the war.
111 *Morpeth Herald*, 1 January 1943, p. 2.
112 *Morpeth Herald*, 1 January 1943, p. 2.
113 *Newcastle Journal*, 5 February 1943, p 3.
114 *Ibid.*
115 *Evening Chronicle*, 5 February 1943, p. 5.
116 *Newcastle Journal*, 5 February 1943, p 3.
117 *Evening Chronicle*, 5 February 1943, p. 5.
118 Pilot Officer Gray's pilot was 21-year-old Flight Sergeant Frederick Joseph Alexander Steel from Carlisle. He was married to Undine Frances Gwilliam Steel and is buried at Gateshead. Tragically, 515 Squadron exchanged their Defiants for the far more effective Beaufighter later that month.
119 *Evening Chronicle*, 15 April 1943, p. 8.

120   *Northern Daily Mail*, 24 May 1943, p. 4.

121   *Evening Chronicle*, 23 July 1943, p. 4.

122   *Evening Chronicle*, 24 July 1943, p. 4.

123   *Evening Chronicle*, 26 July 1943, p. 3. Imprisonment in the Second Division was a condition whereby prisoners were kept away from other classes of prisoners, wore a different uniform and received more mail and visitor access.

124   *Sunderland Echo & Shipping Gazette*, 26 July 1943, p. 5.

125   Admiral Evans, later 1st Baron Mountevans, was a figure of some fame. He had captained the ship which transported Robert Falcon Scott's ill-fated South Pole expedition in 1910-13. Evans had been due to accompany the expedition to the pole as second-in-command but came down with a life-threatening case of scurvy and was not with the party who all died in their attempt. During the First World War he achieved some fame as a destroyer captain before going on to senior command positions within the RN. Appointed as Regional Civil Defence Commissioner for London in 1939 he had also journeyed to Norway after Germany invaded that country. As a personal acquaintance of King Haakon VII he liaised with the monarch before returning to Britain. Raised to the peerage in 1945 he sat in the House of Lords as a Labour peer until his death in 1957.

126   In addition to the two pilots named above five of the dead were: Vliegtuigmaker (equivalent to a Flight Engineer) Rudi Van Den Bron; Matroos (equivalent to an Able Seaman) Daniel Johnannes Kooij; Matroos Arie Willem Van Egmond; Matroos Frans Van Westenbrugge; and Leading Aircraftman Frank Lester Beresford (29). LAC Beresford was an under training Air Gunner. I have been unable to positively identify the remaining two airmen to lose their lives.

127   652 Squadron went on to fly in support of the British army and began operational flights over Normandy on the day after D-Day. C Flight claimed the distinction of taking part in the final shots fired in the European war when it directed artillery fire during the siege of Dunkirk on 7 May 1945.

128   Flying Officer Rossignol was from Washington DC and was a pilot with 20 OTU based at Lossiemouth from where he and his trainee crew took on a training exercise in a Wellington bomber. The aircraft crashed at Pigdon, just outside of Morpeth, after suffering an explosion in mid-air.

129   *Morpeth Herald*, 7 May 1943, p. 4.

130   *Morpeth Herald*, 14 May 1943, p. 4.

131   *Morpeth Herald*, 4 June 1943, p. 3.

132   *Morpeth Herald*, 24 September 1943, p. 4.

133   *Morpeth Herald*, 14 May 1943, p. 4.

134 *Morpeth Herald*, 30 July 1943, p. 2.

135 *Morpeth Herald*, 14 May 1943, p. 4.

136 Private Dixon is buried at Yokohama War Cemetery.

137 *The Journal*, 17 July 1945, p. 2.

138 Sergeant Gray's body lies in Rheinburg War Cemetery, as does that of his crewmate Flight Sergeant Garner (from Staplehurst, Kent). Sergeant Gray's headstone has the following inscription upon it: 'Deep in our hearts A memory is kept Of one we loved And will never forget'. W7876 was one of four losses suffered from 35 Squadron on this night; 40 per cent of the total Halifax losses for the night.

139 *The Journal*, 23 February 1943, p. 4.

140 It is likely that the Lancaster exploded in mid-air and that the pilot was blown from the aircraft but was wearing a seat-type parachute harness enabling him to descend safely. Aside from Pilot Officer Armstrong the deceased were: Sgt Mervyn Jones (Flight Engineer); Flying Officer Frederick Leonard Yates (Air Bomber); Sgt Peter Williams (Wireless Operator/Air Gunner); Sgt Derek Murphy (Mid Upper Air Gunner); and Sgt John Albert Thomas Newton (Rear Air Gunner).

141 The crew were: Pilot Officer A.O. Smuck (Pilot), RCAF; Sgt Foggon; Flying Officer J.J. Kelly (Navigator); Sgt B. Domigan (Air Bomber); Sgt R. Barneveld (Wireless operator/Air Gunner); Sgt D.G. McKay, RCAF (Mid Upper Air Gunner); and Sgt D.L.G. Brown, RCAF (Rear Air Gunner).

142 295 Squadron was formed as part of 38 Group as an airbourne forces squadron. Re-equipped with Albermarles the squadron shared the distinction of dropping the first allied troops on D-Day.

143 *Morpeth Herald*, 18 February 1944, p. 3.

144 The other man who was killed was Battery Sergeant Major Harold Dyke, 510 Coast Regiment, Royal Artillery.

145 An old-fashioned name for Hydrochloric Acid.

146 Lieutenant John Butcher, 142nd Regt., Royal Armoured Corps, was killed on 8 June 1944. He is buried at Bolsena War Cemetery.

147 Petty Officer Stafford was buried at sea and is commemorated on the Chatham Naval Memorial and on the family headstone in Blyth. His father, Bolton Bird Naiden Stafford died in 1946 aged just 55. Born in 1920 Petty Officer Stafford was the eldest son of four siblings.

148 *Evening Chronicle*, 9 June 1944, p. 3.

149 Ironically, just days after this hearing compulsory service in the Home Guard was ended.

150 *Evening Chronicle*, 16 August 1944, p. 4.

151 *Morpeth Herald*, 1 September 1944, p. 1.

152 Lieutenant Stephen Trevor Beckerleg, 3rd (attached to 2nd) Btn, Duke of Cornwall's Light Infantry, was killed on 15 October 1915.

He had been a student at Camborne (Cornwall) School of Mines and had volunteered, aged 19, at the outbreak of war. He is buried at Heat Cemetery, Harbonnieres.

153 *Morpeth Herald*, 8 December 1944, p. 5.

154 *Ibid*.

155 *Morpeth Herald*, 8 December 1944, p. 2.

156 *Morpeth Herald*, 22 December 1944, p. 5.

157 *Morpeth Herald*, 11 May 1945, p. 4.

158 HMS *Blackpool* was a Bangor-class minesweeper which had been launched at the Harland & Wolff yard at Govan in 1940 and served in the English Channel for most of the war. She was transferred to the Norwegian navy in late 1946 becoming the HNoMS *Tarna*.

159 *Morpeth Herald*, 11 May 1945, p. 2.

160 *Morpeth Herald*, 11 May 1945, p. 4.

161 *Ibid*, p. 2.

162 This was a memorable moment for Wing Commander Petre as he had flown with 19 Squadron in 1940.

163 By coincidence both of the pilots were local men. Flight Lieutenant Arthur James Frederick Young (28) was from Jesmond, Newcastle upon Tyne and is commemorated on the Runnymede Memorial while Flight Lieutenant Robert William Robson (26) was from Whitley Bay and is buried in his hometown at Whitley Bay (Hartley South) Cemetery.

164 Both 289 and 291 Squadron were disbanded by the end of the month.

165 Eshott remained in use by 261 MU until 1 January 1948. In the early 1980s, flying returned to Eshott when the Eshott Airfield Flying Club based itself there.

166 261 MU was responsible for the collection and disposal of ground equipment in the north-east and was staffed mainly by civilians with only a few RAF personnel.

167 62 OTU had been joined by 1508 Beam Approach Training Flight in June 1944.

168 They were used to train would be radar operators who would go on to fly in Mosquito night-fighters.

169 The pilot successfully performed a belly-landing near Eshott Farm.

170 80 (French) OTU was combined into the Armee de l'Air in March 1946 while a variety of units followed it to Ouston with the airfield finally being transferred to the Army in 1975. Although no officially known as Albermarle Barracks it is still often referred to by its former name.

171 Those who have read the author's work on *Morpeth in the Great War* (Pen & Sword, 2016) may recall that the firm had a fine record in that conflict too with over fifty men serving and seven being killed including two sons of the firm's directors (Captain C. Swinney, MC, and Lieutenant Norman Swinney).

172 Mr Dippie's brother David had also worked for Swinney's for over fifty
     years as well as being a renowned bellringer who had rung the town's
     bells to celebrate the relief of the siege of Mafeking, the end of the Boer
     War, the end of World War One and many subsequent great events.

173 It had been a peacetime tradition, now defunct, of the section to
     take upwards of 400 Morpethians (mostly unaccompanied children),
     accompanied by the mayor and mayoress, to the pantomime at
     Newcastle. The group was met by a detachment from the Newcastle
     City Police who supervised the unloading, escort and loading of the
     group.

174 The sheep ked is a tick-like bloodsucking fly.

Index